MORMON BOY

A MEMOIR

WARREN DRIGGS

Copyright @ 2019 by Warren Driggs

Published by
Paradise Rim Books
Salt Lake City, UT

ISBN: 978-0-9987795-4-6 (paperback)
eISBN: 978-0-9987795-5-3

Book Design by GKS Creative, Nashville

Library of Congress Information is on file with the Publisher.

A Mormon boy, a Mormon boy,
I am a Mormon boy;
I might be envied by a king,
For I am a Mormon boy.

Also by Warren Driggs

A Tortoise in the Road

Old Scratch

Swimming in Deep Water: A Novel of Joeph Smith

For Scott, Chad, Sarah, and Ben

Preface

I RECENTLY ATTENDED A COCKTAIL PARTY IN New York City. The guests stood clustered in the swanky high-rise apartment overlooking the East River, admiring the spectacular view. They glanced over each other's shoulders while checking out their own reflections in the large windows, touching their hair. Servers with white shirts and black aprons trolled through the crowd with trays of stuffed mushrooms, bacon-wrapped dates, and glasses of chardonnay.

A bald man wearing a dinner jacket and purple pocket square had me cornered, generously sharing his wisdom concerning matters of high finance. He could tell I didn't know much about high finance, so he had much to say. I stood with a wadded-up cocktail napkin in my hand and nodded at timely intervals. I caught him looking at my shoes and a moment later, when he wasn't looking, I lifted my right shoe and buffed it on the back of my left pant leg, and then repeated the task for my left shoe.

We were soon joined by others who'd gravitated to the scent of this wealthy man. The subject of politics came up.

"What we need," one of them in an Italian pinstripe said, "is someone like Mitt Romney." Another man jiggled the ice in his single-malt scotch. "I agree," he said, for he assumed this was a like-minded crowd. "But I think his Mormonism hurts him."

I told them I was also a Mormon, albeit a shirttail one, at best. "I don't know Mitt personally," I said, "but he happens to be my neighbor. In fact, he lives a few doors down from me and I suspect I'm in his Mormon ward."

"You're a Mormon?" one of them asked. I couldn't tell if he was amused or just surprised.

"Well, yes, I once was. In fact, I was born and raised in the church. I went on a two-year Mormon mission and married my high school girlfriend in the Mormon temple."

These men were curious about my Mormonism. Did I have more than one wife? Why did I have a glass of wine in my hand? How many children did I have? And what, pray tell, was the deal with their underwear?

I brought them up to speed on the cornerstones of Mormonism—just a few fun highlights—like the secret gold tablets, the ancient mummy scrolls, the origin of polygamy, and the fact that I was one of 10 children who grew up wondering when Jesus would return from the sky to burn all the wicked people to stubble in the Last Days.

I could also have told them about our bomb shelters and how we were encouraged to stockpile food for the apocalypse, or that my grandmother's family fled to Mexico to avoid being arrested for polygamy. And perhaps I could have clarified that I married my high school girlfriend within weeks of returning from my mission for the church. I hadn't planned to go to college at the time—I was going to be a paint contractor. But after rinsing my hands in turpentine all summer I decided to enroll at the university as a 21-year-old married man, having graduated from high school by the skin of my teeth. It was only then that I was exposed to ideas that would alter my life and belief in Mormonism.

But this was a cocktail party, not a forum for explaining my religious journey. Otherwise I could've told them I no longer maintain my youthful beliefs in Mormon Church doctrine. Nevertheless, those early beliefs, and my extraordinary parents, were the paramount influences of my youth.

"You need to write your story," the man in the Italian pinstripe said. "I think it's fascinating."

I realized he was right; I *did* need to write my story. The story of what it was like to grow up in a devout Mormon family and a nearly all-Mormon community. So here goes.

I know an awful lot about Mormonism. It is generational in my family. My ancestors were our family's original members of the church and made the arduous trek across the midwestern plains and Rocky Mountains, some of them pushing handcarts and others riding in covered wagons pulled by oxen. My childhood was unusual, too, because of my upbringing.

This memoir is about my childhood growing up in Utah as a Mormon boy (my adult life is not nearly as interesting). I was indoctrinated into the curious beliefs of Mormonism, beliefs that did not seem curious to me as a youngster. In fact, I continued to believe in Angel Moroni, and all the other Mormon angels who visited the earth, long after my belief in the Easter Bunny had expired. Indeed, it wasn't until I was in my 20s that I emerged from my cocoon and developed an understanding that the earth probably wasn't just 6,000 years old, that the Garden of Eden probably wasn't in western Missouri, and that Jesus probably wouldn't descend upon the mid-west United States for his long awaited Second Coming.

This is my story, not Mormonism's. It is difficult for me to reflect on my childhood, however, and not see how intertwined they were. Of course, not all of my childhood memories directly involve the church, but it is there, always, as the backdrop that prejudiced my early views of the world.

This is not the sort of memoir where the protagonist gallantly overcomes hardship—a story of angst, addiction, abuse, and abandonment. I was not the victim of sexual or physical abuse, childhood neglect, or crippling poverty. I didn't battle a debilitating illness or any particular tragedy. My childhood was happy and good. And neither is this story the rags to riches one that you didn't see coming, nor the tale of someone who has risen to dazzling heights of fame, for my talents are modest.

My history, like any history, requires an investigation that is handicapped by my flawed memory and inescapable bias. My childhood stories are not individually determinative, but the collection of them are the threads that stitched together my early philosophies. Indeed, my past and current beliefs can be found in those very seams.

How I wish I could go back in time and interview my adolescent self! I imagine the absolute *confidence* in that boy's unexamined beliefs, the emphatic *righteousness* of his convictions! I'd be curious to see the look on that adolescent face when I, the ghost of his future self, told him he would eventually kill off most of those beliefs—a systematic, deliberate, and premeditated assassination of the faith he cherished. He would have been shocked because, back then, the basis of his beliefs had not yet been tested, had not yet faced the storms of science, adulthood, and experience. He hadn't faced a single headwind, a single gust of contradiction or hypocrisy. The shelter of his religious community had seen to that.

And now, I neither wish to apologize for my early beliefs, nor endorse them. And neither do I wish to disparage anyone else's beliefs, especially those of my amazing siblings and friends, many of whom maintain their belief in Mormonism's miraculous tale by tapping into their deep reservoir of faith. I am happy for them, though that reservoir has evaporated for me.

All I wish to do is tell my story.

1

MY FIRST CHILDHOOD MEMORY WAS RUNNING AWAY from home, so I might as well start there. For the record, running away hadn't been my idea. I was only 4-years old and was quite satisfied with my life the way it was. This act of utter disobedience would never have occurred to me if not for my 5-year-old brother who felt justified in running away because of some unremembered injustice. He dragged me along as a co-conspirator because I was a pleaser. Whether or not his response to the injustice required such a dramatic act, I cannot say.

I have earlier memories, but they are just glimpses. There was the girl across the street on Emerson Avenue whose head was twice the size it should have been, getting Zorro's autograph, and the duck flying around our living room, having been set loose by the Navajo boy who lived with my cousins.

My memory is not crisp when I try to recollect my mom's reaction to us running away (I will just assume here that my dad never knew. After all, he didn't even know my birthdate—my mom had to remind him about things like that). Was she mad? Did she pace the kitchen floor, worried sick over our safety?

Or did she even know we'd escaped out the bedroom window? We'd packed a few pieces of bread and made it all the way to Westminster College, up a very steep hill nearly one mile away, before my brother decided we had emphatically made our point.

I'm the third of 10 children. I've read about birth order and how rank affects your personality. Now, I'm not especially cynical about this sort of analysis, but I don't think we were a poster family for psychological conformity. I was not a first born, last born, or only child. So, yeah, I was a middle child, but that put me in the same mix with Danny, Jane, Paul, David, Ben, Matt, and Steve. And we're all different. (I suppose Andy fits the mold of a last born, but he wasn't spoiled to the point of being helpless. None of us were spoiled. And Julie, who was the first born, never had a strong need for approval.) We were different, our family.

Take my dad, Leonard. There was no one, and I mean no one, like my dad. He was optimistic by nature, irrationally so, as if a waitress followed him around wherever he went, day and night, topping his half-full glass to the brim. And then there was my mom, Helen, who felt obliged to tamp down our egos, for when my dad's glass had been topped off, he'd be liable to say anything. "No, honey," she said after my dad heard me sing and promptly declared me to be the best singer he'd ever heard, "I hate to tell you this, but you probably won't make the Tabernacle Choir." Or the time my dad assured me I'd probably play for the Yankees one day after striking out twice in three times at bat in Little League. "Listen, honey, your dad . . . well, your dad thinks the world of you kids, but let's be realistic."

My parents had different styles, dramatically different. When I was older and had just passed the bar exam (presumably by a whisker, for I was a mediocre student), my dad told anyone who would listen that I'd probably be appointed to the Supreme Court any day. Failing that, I'd probably become the President. My mom's response to my success was a little different. I'd gone to her house for lunch a few months after my swearing in and I was wearing a tie that I'd just bought at Nordstrom. It cost $100, an extravagant purchase for me, and I was feeling quite special. My mom was in her sewing room when I came into the kitchen. "You look handsome today, honey," she said from the side of her mouth that wasn't clamped down over three or four pins. I thanked her and then proudly pointed out my new tie. "Oh, that *is* lovely," she said.

Yes, I thought I was really something, a lawyer and everything. My mom, who was still holding a pair of scissors, approached me to inspect the tie more closely. Then, without batting an eye, she lifted her scissors and cut the tie in half. "It's only a tie, honey," she said. "Now it's time to get over yourself."

I don't mean to suggest that my mom wasn't proud of us. She was. She just didn't go for shallow achievement. After fixing me lunch that day, she said "You know, honey, I'm sorry about your tie, really I am. You are the most amazing young man I know, but it has nothing to do with a stupid tie. That's just window dressing."

My parents came from very different backgrounds but they had one thing in common: their devotion to the church. And when I say the church, I mean The Church, the only true one on the face of the earth. Their belief in Mormonism was hardcore, on the verge of fanaticism. Their roots in the church went way back, all the way to the founder, Joseph Smith. Their great-grandparents were early Mormon pioneers who made the bumpy trek in covered wagons across the country to the Salt Lake Valley.

What was it like to grow up Mormon in Salt Lake City? First of all, you should understand that Mormonism is more than a religion, more than a strain of faith. It is a way of life. The church directly influenced what I ate, what I wore, what I drank, what movies I watched, and how I spent my free time. Our challenge was not to be popular, but to be holy. Try being both popular and holy at the same time. It's tough.

In my little enclave, everyone I knew was a Mormon. They weren't weird either. At least I didn't think so. For example, I didn't think it was weird that we didn't drink coffee, or that my great-great grandfather had a slew of wives. I didn't even think it was weird that I would become a God one day. You read that right—I was taught that if I behaved and was a good member of the church that I would eventually become a God and have my own planet. This wasn't meant to be dismissive of God, of course. His name was Elohim and we loved him. He was God, after all. But Mormons had a saying that everyone memorized early on. It went like this: "As man is, God once was. As God is, man may become." This was the concept of eternal progression.

Therefore, God was once just like me and eventually graduated to Godhood, and I was on the same track. So, there was a lot on the line compelling me to behave. We had other incentives, of course, but this was the big one. It doesn't get much bigger.

I can now understand how all this God business must have rubbed people the wrong way. Of course, most people don't think they are on the God track the way I did. They think it is the height of insanity, the epitome of arrogance, or the gall of blasphemy (or, more likely, all three of them at once). But I wasn't the only person who figured he'd be a God someday. My dentist, doctor, school teacher, and garbage collector all thought the same thing. And so did my barber, scoutmaster, and Little League coach, to say nothing of the Governor, our two United States Senators, and our Congressmen. It was a mainstream belief in my town. (You'll notice there are no women on the list. That is because only men could become Gods. A woman, provided she was married to a Mormon man, could become a Goddess, but she wouldn't get her own planet—she'd just help her husband manage his.)

We could have strutted around bragging about it, but we didn't—we didn't try to rub it in people's faces. You never heard Senator Orrin Hatch proclaim on the floor of the United States Senate that the Mormon prophet had more authority than the President or the Speaker of the House, but you could bet he believed it. We tried to be humble and keep our opinions to ourselves. (Well, that is until we turned 19 and went on our missions, when we basically told everyone who didn't join our church to pack their bags because they'd be going to hell. This was meant in the most Christian way, of course.)

That sort of expectation—the embryonic God syndrome— has an effect on you. How could it not? I knew we were right and everyone else was in the loony bin. I mean, after all, we *were* the Chosen People. This conviction was based entirely on what my parents and Sunday School teachers told me (and what *their* parents and Sunday School teachers had told *them*). This certainty of belief was the bedrock of my life, so much so that I didn't even need to think about it. The thinking had already been done. I didn't vet my beliefs, not even once. I do not confess this boastfully.

My friends and I snickered at the madness, the outright *absurdity*, of Mohammed's claim to have seen an angel. Or how about those Catholics and all the angelic saints they had? *Angels?* Those people were nuts! Of course, our angels were the real deal, not a bunch of phony Catholic ones.

My fair community was as comfortably homogenous as it could be, full of well-behaved Saints. That's what we called members of the church: Saints. We weren't trying to be arrogant about it, we were just Saints. And everyone who wasn't a member of the church was called a Gentile. Obviously, Saints were good and Gentiles were not. However, to be fair, Gentiles weren't necessarily irredeemable. In fact, some of them were perfectly nice and friendly. They just didn't have the truth like we did, that's all. Catholics, Protestants, Jews, Lutherans, atheists; you name it, they were all Gentiles (only in Utah could a Jew be a full-blown Gentile). At the time, I felt fortunate to be living in mostly a Gentile Free Zone.

When I was in first grade our teacher, Mrs. Anderson, asked if anyone could name any of the Presidents. Mark Layton, a boy in my neighborhood, raised his hand. "I can name them, in order," he boasted. Mrs. Anderson was duly impressed and asked him to stand in front of the class and reel them off. "First there was Joseph Smith, then Brigham Young, then John Taylor, then Wilford Woodruff." I remember nodding along, checking his accuracy (and he was spot on so far), but Mrs. Anderson interrupted him before he could name all 13 of them. "Mark, I meant the Presidents of the United States." He petered out pretty quickly after naming George Washington and Abraham Lincoln, and he only got those because of the paper silhouettes of their profiles hanging above the blackboard. There was simply no way he could get Millard Fillmore.

That's how Mormon my first-grade class was. That's how Mormon my whole community was. And that's how Mormon my own family was, too. Going way back.

My pioneer ancestors were dirt poor when they finally settled in the west. Unfortunately, my dad's side of the family stayed that way. His grandparents had migrated to the Teton Valley in eastern Idaho where they tried to grow strawberries in a town that would come to be named after my great grandfather: Driggs, Idaho. This was tough work, growing strawberries where the cold wind gushed down from Canada and the annual growing season lasted about 48 hours. My dad's early years were marked by poverty, growing up in a log cabin without running water or reliable chinking. He'd regale us with stories of his childhood where the central theme was always love; love of his parents, love of his siblings, love of the church. The point was that he felt lucky to have been born into such an amazing family, and I got that, I did, but the backstory was always poverty.

When my dad was only 7, his father died of pneumonia, leaving a widow, six kids, and a small patch of strawberries. They ate milkweeds for dinner and had a dirt roof. They'd trudge through the snow and ice to use the outhouse. But they were happy, at least according to my dad. And I believed him. But eating weeds? They couldn't last, and shortly after my grandfather's death, my grandmother moved with the children to Salt Lake City.

When my grandma died four decades later, we loaded her pine casket into the back of my cousin's old pickup truck. The bed of the pickup wasn't long enough to accommodate the casket so we had to prop the end of the casket up at an angle onto the top of the tailgate for the five-hour drive from Salt Lake City to Driggs, Idaho where she was buried. I'm sure my poor grandma's head was squished into the top of the casket by the time we arrived.

My mom, Helen, also had an impressive Mormon pedigree. She grew up in a small bungalow in Sugarhouse which is on Salt Lake City's east side, the classier side of the tracks. Her father was a lawyer. She was a private person and less inclined to tell childhood stories, and when she did, they weren't nearly as fantastic as the ones my dad told. She'd contracted polio as a child and spent several months quarantined in the hospital where even her parents couldn't visit her. I often wonder how this shaped her, waving to her parents through the hospital window on Christmas. She dragged her leg for the rest of her life as a result of the polio. It wasn't dramatic, this leg dragging, and she never once complained about it. In fact, many people didn't even know about her disability because she hid it so well under her collection of muumuus.

You must know that my mom was straight-laced to a T (she walked out of *Ghostbusters* when they swore and would have passed out had she known that I'd sneaked into a showing of *The Graduate* at the local drive-in). My mom was obedient, period. Obedience was her creed. If the church leaders had told her to stand on her head in the kitchen for 15 minutes every Thursday afternoon for reasons unknown, she would have done it. To her, you didn't question. You doubted your doubts. Her devotion to her faith never wavered. Her only phobia was sin. (Well, that and mice. A mouse ran across her pillow while she was being quarantined for polio and she'd been petrified of the creatures ever since. She passed this particular phobia on to me.)

Even though my mom was ultra-conservative, I don't wish to paint her as dowdy. She wasn't dowdy. In fact, she was rather hip in her mother-of-10-children-straight-as-an-arrow way. She was a hoot and could relate to everyone, even common sinners. My teenage friends would always come to my house to hang out with my mom, even when I wasn't around. "Let's go talk to Helen," they'd say. "We gotta tell her what Howard did. She'd get a kick out of it," they'd say. They opened up to her for some reason, divulging information that they wouldn't share with any other adult.

The same woman who walked out of *Ghostbusters* was a card-shark (but she had an on-again off-again aversion to face cards because they were wicked for reasons that were never fully explained to me). If she didn't like a card, she'd just pick another one. "I'm your mother and I'll cheat if I feel like it." Or there was the time we were playing Pinochle on a motorhome trip. If she didn't like a particular card, she'd roll down the window and throw it out, even though I know she felt bad about the littering.

Or there was the time later in her life when she was riding one of those Jazzy scooters like you see at Walmart because her polio made it difficult to walk. One of her grandkids accidently sprayed ketchup on her face, hair, and blouse. She immediately pretended to be a crazy disabled person, pawing at the air with one hand and smearing the ketchup all over her face with the other one. She even dipped a few French fries into the globs of ketchup in her hair and ate them. This was my mom, a fascinating contradiction of radical *and* conservative. She was the one who would lecture me about an R-rated movie, then cut off my tie, and then make me sit down and chat about the Oscars.

In any case, my mom was rigid about following the commandments. She'd constantly remind us about the devil and his wicked shenanigans. "Now you listen to me, Buster. Only the devil is up past midnight," she'd say. But then again, I remember when my own children were pre-teens. It was about midnight and we were all in bed. I heard a car honking in our circular driveway and peered out the window. It was my mom's Pontiac. I went downstairs and out to her car. The interior car light came on when I opened her passenger door. "What's the matter, Mom? Is everything okay?" She was wearing her powder-blue bathrobe and house slippers. "Hurry, go get the kids," she said. "We're going toilet papering!" When I asked if she was serious, she said, "Of course I'm serious. Now quit being such a goodie-two-shoes and go wake up the kids." I looked into her backseat and saw about 20 rolls of toilet paper. That was my mom.

My dad was a lot of fun too. I went to his office as a teenager one morning to borrow $10 to go skiing (my dad had become an insurance salesman by then). "Can I come, too?" he asked, sitting behind his desk in a suit and tie. "Uh, sure dad, but we were gonna leave, like, right now." This was not a problem for my dad. "Cancel my appointments," he said to his secretary on his way out the door. I asked him if he wanted to ride in the front seat. "No, that's Eric's spot. I can fit in back here." He slid our stuff out of the way in the back seat and squeezed into a spot better suited to a toddler. "Oh, yeah, this is plenty of room. We're gonna have a great time!"

I asked him if he wanted to swing by the house to change out of his suit and tie. "Nah," he said, "I'll be fine." He only asked to stop at a rental shop near the mouth of the canyon so he could rent a pair of skis and boots. Toward the end of the day he paused, looked quizzically at me, and asked why I wasn't in school, as if it hadn't occurred to him until that moment that I was sluffing. I told him I had my school work handled (which was a bald-faced lie). "Okay then," he said, "I trust your judgment. Now, come on, I'll race you to the bottom!" I will never forget my dad that day, snow-plowing down the slopes of Solitude Ski Resort in a suit and tie. That was my dad.

———

My dad was an auto mechanic when he met my mom. He was handsome, unusually so, with the bluest eyes I'd ever seen. That this grease monkey with chapped knuckles and dirty fingernails would land my mom was a testament to his charisma. I often wonder what her parents must have thought about their 17-year-old daughter dropping out of high school to marry an auto mechanic from the poor side of town. But if you knew my dad, you'd want to marry him too.

They pledged to have a dozen children because Mormonism taught them to "multiply and replenish the earth." They took this to heart. You see, Mormons believe there are multitudes of spirits up in heaven waiting to come down to earth and get a physical body. So, it was charitable to make it happen for them, and utterly selfish to preclude it by using birth control (to say nothing of how potentially sinful it was). You might get away with the rhythm method, in a pinch, but it made no sense to risk God's wrath. Sex was purposeful. Ten children and at least two miscarriages in 18 years. You can't say they were slackers, and for that I am grateful.

2

I HAVE TWO SISTERS AND SEVEN BROTHERS. Each one of my brothers has a Biblical name, and then there's me: Warren. There is no Warren in the Bible. I was one of the first sons too, so it's not like my parents had run out of New and Old Testament names. They'd already used Daniel for my older brother, but after I was born they still had a stable of leftover Bible names they could have used. However, they skipped me and used them for my younger brothers Paul, David, Benjamin, Matthew, Steven, and Andrew.

I didn't like my name as a kid. For starters, the fattest boy in school was also named Warren. He wore coke-bottle glasses, suspenders, and a pocket protector. Perhaps he couldn't control his weight, or wardrobe, so I should've cut him some slack, but he picked his nose and ate them like it was going out of style. And there was really no excuse for that. People got us confused. And then there was Warren Jeffs, the fundamentalist Mormon polygamist who is now in prison for marrying about 20 teenage girls at once, impregnating them all. I felt like I was starting behind the eight ball.

Back then, Mormons were (and still are, in some circles) known for polygamy. "Yeah, aren't they the ones out there in Utah who have a dozen wives or something?" It always annoyed me to hear that, like Utah was in a different galaxy. We weren't polygamists, people! Well, actually, we were and we weren't. To make sense of that, I need to explain more about how I was going to be a God one day, and at the same time go back and outline some Mormon history.

See, God told Joseph Smith that if we get baptized and keep all the commandments, we can become a God and be awarded a deed to our very own planet. Not too bad, right? But obviously if you were a God and had your own planet, you'd want to populate it, wouldn't you? It'd make no sense to have an empty planet. What would be the point? That's when God told Joseph that he needed to have as many children as possible so he could lord over them one day. Naturally, you'd need a lot of wives in order to populate a town or small village, much less an entire planet. So, that was the gist of it, at least the way it was explained to me. (To be fair to the more cynical, another explanation is that Joseph had been caught having sex with the teenage maid, Fanny Alger, and came up with the new polygamy commandment on the fly.)

The early Mormons weren't very popular with the townsfolk in upstate New York where it all began. To begin with, there was all the God talk. After all, it probably wouldn't sit too well with you if Horace, your neighbor down the street, told you that he was going to become a God and you were going to hell. So, no, this God business hadn't resonated with the locals. But when the Mormons then doubled down with plural wives, well, the neighbors went ballistic. Who *were* these guys? They grabbed their pitchforks and torches and drove the Mormons out of New

York, and then Ohio, and then Missouri, and finally Illinois. The Mormons had had enough of all this wicked persecution so they packed their bags and headed west on their covered-wagon trek across the plains in early spring, 1847.

Several months later, they finally rolled into a desolate basin next to a huge salty lake. By this time, Brigham Young had taken over from Joseph Smith who'd been shot dead in an Illinois jail cell by a gang of unruly bandits (Mormons insist he'd been framed). Let's face it, Brigham was tired—they all were—so he declared that they'd walked far enough. They would settle in this basin. And so they did.

The first year was bleak because the valley was basically a desert and the Mormon pioneers didn't have much to work with. They planted crops and crossed their fingers. It all worked out reasonably well until the Cricket Plague, for not long after they planted their second year of crops, the Mormons watched in horror as massive swarms of crickets descended like the plague of locusts prophesied in the Bible. The crickets ate their way through the corn and cabbage seeds, devouring them. The Mormons were on the brink of disaster and were praying like crazy, when suddenly they looked up to the sky to see their salvation arrive from above. It wasn't Jesus returning from the heavens to save them, it was seagulls. Thousands of them. The seagulls swooped down on the crickets. When the seagulls' bellies were full, they drank water, regurgitated, and went back for more. They ate for two weeks until there wasn't a cricket to be found, and thus the Mormons were saved.

The seagull was eventually named the official state bird.

Once they were finally rid of the crickets, things settled down and the Mormons lived happily in the Salt Lake Valley, doing their thing with polygamy outside the official borders of the United

States. Brigham was especially giddy, for he was the king of this desert kingdom and had over 50 wives. Not only that, but he had at least 56 children. 56. Let that sink in for a moment. Can you imagine the bedtime routine? And how about the middle-child syndrome in *that* family?

Brigham was the gatekeeper in deciding who was allowed to marry whom. He tended to dibs the prettiest women for himself, which can't come as a shocker. Indeed, it seems sensible. But, to be fair, he also quite charitably married a few old maids in their 40s. In fact, he married one 40-year-old woman and then secretly married her teenage her daughter a few weeks later.

Generally speaking, the more righteous you were, the more wives you were allowed. Brigham decided, in an effort to be consistent, that it also made sense for him to decide which men were the most righteous. I can imagine this made him popular with the men in town. I'll bet the guys down at the hardware store and livery stables laughed at all his jokes and asked him if he'd lost weight, or where he shopped for those sporty clothes he wore. Geez, Brigham, do you work out?

That's when the Feds started pestering them about polygamy. The Mormons blew them off, spurning the Union. Rumors and threats of secession swirled a decade before it became a popular thing to do in the deep south. "Mind your own danged business," the Mormons said. "What, you've never heard of the Constitution? There's this thing called Freedom of Religion, so butt out," they said.

The United States army was dispatched to Utah to corral the Mormons back into the fold and quash this outrageous affront to a civilized society. There was a stand-off between the Mormons and the U.S. Army which basically ended when the troops were needed to fight in the Civil War. The Mormons had outlasted them.

Three decades later, the Mormons, who'd previously thumbed their noses at the United States, had a change of heart and desperately wanted to gain official statehood. The Feds said it'd be a cold day in hell unless they abandoned polygamy. So, they finally did. Sort of.

I say "sort of" because groups of devout Mormons ignored the new anti-polygamy law, refusing to turn a blind eye to what God had explicitly commanded. They claimed this anti-polygamy nonsense was merely a law of *man* and they only followed laws of God. My grandmother's family promptly hit the road for Mexico where they could live God's laws in peace without the damned government sticking its nose into their business over who could sleep with whom, and how many wives a man could have. In fact, my grandmother was born in Mexico, along with Mitt Romney's father. They all moved back to the United States when Poncho Villa drove them out of Mexico, once and for all.

Once all the Mormons were safely back in the states, a few offshoots broke away from the main church and moved into other communities here in Utah and Arizona where they still practice polygamy today. Those are the people you see at Costco in their homemade prairie dresses. They continue to proudly declare themselves to be Mormon. In fact, they claim to be the purest Mormons of all because they didn't sell out to the Feds.

By the time I came along Mormons no longer practiced polygamy, and I didn't think about it much when I was growing up because it was too remote and too weird. And if I ever did think about it, it was under the influence of a certain religious spin. I'd been taught that my ancestors begrudgingly practiced polygamy because they wanted to *help* women, not enslave them. These polygamist men were essentially heroes, taking in young women who needed support. "What, you think they *wanted* to have sex with them?" my Sunday School teacher asked. Absolutely not. They did it to help the poor young things. (I submit that, however it worked in the past, it doesn't work very well for those women and girls today. If you've ever been to a Walmart in southern Utah, you'll know what I mean.)

I don't personally know any polygamists in Salt Lake City, but they're around, all right. Maybe not the hardcore ones who shun modernity—the ones who think modern Mormons are lascivious with their too-short shorts and the way some women tuck their sacred undergarments into their shoulders so they can wear their Lululemon. This staunch bunch thinks half the girls at BYU are harlots while the rest of the country thinks they are prudes. These fundamentalists might be the only ones on earth who think a place like Salt Lake City is Sin City—the Sodom and Gomorrah of our day.

The polygamists I've seen look sad, like they're obliged to lug the burden of their righteousness around like a yoke, as if the weight of the world's collective sin has wrung every ounce of joy from them. I feel sorry for them, especially the children. The young girls who wear gray little prairie dresses that cover everything but their white socks and scuffed Reeboks will probably be married off to old men with hair coming out of their ears. And the boys? Many of them will be shipped out of town with a one-way bus ticket once they're old enough to compete for the affections of the girls. I try to smile at them but they won't make eye contact with me. They lower their gaze or turn their head. I presume they pity me because of my bleak eternal prognosis, doomed no doubt because I turned my back on God and sold out to the authority of the Feds.

Mormons believe the polygamy commandment will be renewed in full force in heaven, after they die, because it's still on the books and was only temporarily suspended to humor the government. When I was younger, I pictured myself up in heaven surrounded by my adoring harem, pollinating all of them with my seed, one at a time. There was a brief time in my teens when this fantasy alone kept me on the straight and narrow.

I can't speak for all Mormon men, of course I can't, but I know some cling to the hope that they'll be given a bundle of wives in heaven. And God knows they'll need them to populate their planets.

3

MORMONS HAVE THEIR ANGELS, LOTS OF THEM in fact. But one angel in particular merits special attention because this angel got the whole thing going. His name was Moroni. He's the one who told Joseph Smith where the golden tablets were buried, the same secret tablets Joseph then used to write The Book of Mormon, the church's most sacred and important scripture.

I saw *The Book of Mormon* Broadway play one time in New York. I thought it was pretty funny (most Mormons would be horrified). However, I thought it skipped through the story of Angel Moroni too quickly, so quickly in fact that you'd miss the whole point of his relevance to your salvation if you weren't paying attention. So, here is the more complete version:

There was a Jew named Lehi who lived with his family in Jerusalem about 2,500 years ago. Lehi was a good man who loved God, and because he was so faithful, God repaid him with a vision that would come to save his life. In this vision, God forewarned him that the people in Jerusalem were walking on awfully thin ice because of their wickedness and that he (God) would probably need to fire-bomb the city to clean out all the corruption and abominations happening there. He told Lehi to build a few boats and skedaddle with his family across the great seas. He promised Lehi that he would provide a magic compass to lead the way (this magic compass was a literal godsend because they didn't have reliable maps back then).

Lehi did as he was told and built the boats. Then he and his family sailed, and kept sailing, until they bumped into land. That land, as it turns out, was somewhere in North America, probably down by Mexico (but no one is certain—it wasn't like Plymouth Rock with a monument or anything).

Lehi had two sons—one was named Nephi and the other was named Laman. They were good kids for the most part, but then Laman started acting out. In fact, God was so upset with Laman and his carousing that he cursed him with a dark skin (you will see as I tell the story that God was fairly liberal with the skin curse). This curse upset Laman so much that he went off on his own with his darkened skin and started raising havoc. He infected his children and all his posterity not only with the darker skin, but also with his wicked lifestyle.

Over the next centuries, both the white people (Nephi's posterity who came to be known as Nephites) and the dark-skinned people (Laman's posterity who came to be known as Lamanites) fought. They fought against each other in one war after another. Their respective populations grew and migrated north, up the eastern seaboard of what is now the United States. Finally, the two civilizations had the battle of all battles, a fight to the finish, for each side was determined to exterminate the other. This epic battle occurred about 400 A.D. in what is now upstate New York, fairly close to Rochester.

The military General for the Nephites (the white people) was named Moroni, an impressive specimen of strength and virtue (to say nothing of his military skills). However, the Lamanites (the dark-skinned people) had more soldiers and they just kept coming, killing off the Nephites left and right. Moroni was eventually the only white man left standing (so maybe his military skills weren't so impressive after all). Because he was the General and also the spiritual leader of the Nephites, Moroni kept the history of his people with him at all times. This history had been etched on golden tablets because they didn't have paper back then. Each prophet over the preceding centuries had etched on a tablet what he thought was important and passed it on, so by the time Moroni received them there was a thick stack of gold tablets, maybe eight inches tall. It had presumably been a burden to lug these heavy tablets around for all those years, especially when battling the Lamanites, but it was worth it because the tablets contained the only recorded history of the people who lived in North America.

Now, Moroni knew he couldn't single-handedly fend off the entire Lamanite army and would soon be stabbed to death. So, at the last minute, when no one was looking, he dug a hole in the ground and buried the stack of gold tablets. He did it in the nick of time too, for he was slaughtered like the rest of his white people a few minutes later. Fortunately, the dark-skinned Lamanites didn't see him bury the gold.

The gold tablets lay buried in the hillside, untouched, for nearly 1,500 years.

We now fast-forward to 1824 in a small village in upstate New York. A teenage boy named Joseph Smith was fast asleep in the upstairs bedroom of the family cabin that he shared with his five brothers. Without warning, the room became bright, so bright in fact that it hurt Joseph's eyes to open them. Naturally, he woke up (his brothers didn't, for some reason) to see an angel hovering in mid-air next to his bed, about a foot off the floor.

The angel introduced himself as Moroni. He told Joseph that he had lived on earth hundreds of years earlier and was now an angel. He told young Joseph about the secret golden tablets that he had buried in the hillside shortly before he was stabbed to death. He told Joseph that he would show him where the tablets were buried, but only on the condition that Joseph not show them to anyone else. Joseph wisely agreed. Moroni actually appeared to him three times that night, repeating the exact same message, word for word. Joseph was re-awakened each time with this incredible tale.

Shortly thereafter, Joseph sneaked off to the secret hiding spot where he and Moroni had agreed to meet up. Moroni pointed to the spot that was now overgrown with foliage. The angel watched as Joseph dug and found a stone box about two feet deep. Inside the box was the stack of gold tablets. There was also a pair of magic spectacles in the box that Moroni told Joseph would be necessary because the ancient etching on the tablets needed to be translated. The spectacles would magically transform the ancient writing into modern-day English. It was unclear who put the spectacles in the box before Moroni was stabbed, but whoever it was must have assumed that the person who would eventually dig them up all those years later would need them. Whatever the reason, that part was never explained to me.

Joseph's assignment was to translate the tablets using the magic spectacles, but he wasn't allowed to show the tablets (or the spectacles) to anyone, not even his parents. In fact, Joseph said the angel emphatically told him that if anyone else saw them, that person would be struck dead on the spot. Naturally, Joseph's friends and family members were itching to see the gold tablets he spoke of, but they didn't dare risk it.

Joseph slaved away at the translation. Once he was finished, the Angel Moroni came back to retrieve the tablets (and magic spectacles) and whisk them back to heaven before anyone else could see them. The finished translation was called The Book of Mormon, Mormon being Moroni's father and the spiritual leader of his people before Moroni took over. Joseph was so impressed with the chapter Mormon had written that he named the book after him. It is assumed that his son, Moroni, took no offense.

After they'd slaughtered all the white people, the dark-skinned Lamanites continued to live in the area of the last great battle for several more centuries. In fact, these were the Indians that Columbus discovered when he sailed over on the Santa Maria about a thousand years later. Therefore, technically speaking, "Lamanites" are the correct name for Native American Indians as far as Mormons are concerned. People who don't know the story might refer to them as Navajos, Cherokees, and Apaches, but Mormons know they are Lamanites. (Actually, this is only said when Mormons are talking to other Mormons, because it would be too inconvenient to tell the whole story every time a Mormon spoke to someone who had never heard of a Lamanite.)

If you add all this up it means Native American Indians are actually Jewish, but most people aren't aware of that. Come to think of it, as a direct descendant of Nephi, I guess that also made me a Jew. I recently asked a Jewish friend of mine what he thought about that. Of course, he thought I was joking, but in fairness to him, he hadn't read The Book of Mormon.

I wasn't a big reader as a child. In fact, one of very few books I read was The Book of Mormon and I only did so because my dad promised me a lemon meringue pie from Marie Callender's if I did. It was tortuous—all those Thee's, Thou's, and Thus Sayeth's. The only parts I liked were the sword fights and battle scenes. I had probably missed the point, because the bloody battles are just a part of it, sprinkled here and there between the sermons, which are vital.

Perhaps the most important part of the book is the chapter where Jesus came to the American continent after he died on the cross. Most people don't know that because most people haven't read The Book of Mormon. Now, everyone agrees that Jesus was put into a tomb for three days after he was crucified. But what most people don't realize is that he didn't spend his time in the tomb just napping and twiddling his thumbs; he used that time to come to the American continent to tell the Nephites and Lamanites about the gospel.

There is a dramatic scene toward the end of the book where Jesus descends from the sky and all the First Americans naturally fall to their knees in wonder. Jesus didn't have enough time to tell them everything he wanted them to know, but he did give them the gist of his new gospel, including highlights from the Sermon on the Mount. The Nephites and Lamanites saw and felt the nail holes in his hands and feet. Then Jesus ascended back up into heaven (or perhaps he went back to the tomb for the rest of his stay, I was never 100% clear on that).

Anyway, it took me about two grueling months but I finally finished reading the entire Book of Mormon. I'm not sure if I felt more enlightened. I really did it for the pie. When at last I had it, however, my brothers descended upon the pie like the Lamanites descended upon poor Moroni. This was a blatant injustice because they'd only read bits and pieces of the Book of

Mormon themselves, and only as part of family scripture reading time. I think I wound up with one measly piece of pie, hardly enough to have justified reading the whole book. This entire episode might have given Aesop enough fodder to write another fable about the boys who ate the pie of another.

Despite the pie debacle, I also read other sacred Mormon scripture including The Book of Abraham, perhaps Mormonism's second most important treatise. The Book of Abraham is a book that was translated from ancient mummy scrolls. Joseph Smith's luck at discovering the buried communications of the ancients, and his skill at translating them, might've been somewhat remarkable, but just try to remember that Joseph translated The Book of *Mormon* from the stack of gold tablets he found buried in the hillside, and he translated The Book of *Abraham* a few years later from ancient parchments rolled up like high school diplomas that were found buried next to some Egyptian mummies. These were two different discoveries.

See, there was a traveling exhibit of Egyptian mummies making the rounds in the back of a covered wagon in the area where Joseph Smith and his small band of Mormons lived a few years after Joseph got the church up and running. These ancient Egyptian mummies looked like all mummies do, wrapped in gauze that was beginning to fray at the edges. Each mummy came with its own scroll. These scrolls had been buried in the tombs alongside the mummies and were to be used by each mummy to introduce himself to the afterlife, sort of an introductory calling card to gain passage to the next life.

Anyway, no one could read what was on each of these ancient scrolls. It was basically a bunch of unintelligible hieroglyphics, and they didn't have access to the Rosetta Stone (or the magic spectacles which Moroni had taken back to heaven). However, Joseph said he could translate the scrolls because he had the special power to decode these hieroglyphics, having mastered the technique with the gold tablets a few years earlier.

Joseph hunkered down over the scrolls to decipher them. He was thrilled to discover that one of the mummies (there were four of them) turned out to be Abraham from the Bible, unbeknownst to the mummy's owner. *The* one and only Abraham. This was an amazing stroke of good fortune! Abraham's translated scroll became known as The Book of Abraham, and only the Mormons can claim it. The good news for me, as a kid, was that this book wasn't nearly as long as The Book of Mormon. So, while I didn't get an entire pie for reading it, it wasn't as arduous a chore.

I swore the next book I read would be more entertaining, and the Hardy Boys mystery series was certainly that. Those boys solved all sorts of mysteries and got out of a lot of scrapes. The more I thought about it, the Hardy Boys were a lot like Joseph Smith, always trying to get out of a jam. Fortunately, they always did, whereas Joseph wasn't as lucky. As I previously mentioned, he was shot to death in a bloody gun battle while holed up in jail awaiting trial for treason, among other charges. He was only 39 years old when he died, and he left a lot of devastated Saints behind, including 38 lonely wives.

———

Mormons have a special place in their hearts for Native American Indians (aka Lamanites) because of their shared heritage. Maybe that's why the church started the Indian Placement Program. Remember how there was a young Navajo boy living with my cousins and he let a duck loose in our living room? His name was Frankie. My aunt Eloise and uncle Dick took him in under the church program which was designed to bring culture to these disadvantaged kids, basically to turn them into young Republicans.

The Mormon prophet promised that the skin of these Indian children would turn a lighter shade once they had been removed from their families on the reservations in Arizona and placed into Mormon homes. The skin curse would gradually subside as they began to accept the true gospel and abandoned their backward ways. As a young boy, I figured any sensible Navajo would jump at the chance of that. The church eventually discontinued this program because it wasn't working.

I don't know what became of Frankie. Maybe he's back on the reservation, or maybe he's unrecognizable to them now. My best guess is he's in therapy somewhere.

4

WHEN I WAS A KID I WAS CONSTANTLY on the lookout for either the Second Coming or a Russian invasion. It was even money which would come first. I ultimately decided the Russians were a more imminent threat because we'd been looking for the Second Coming for over 150 years, ever since Joseph Smith said it was nigh at hand. It didn't seem that nigh to me. In the meantime, there were the Russians to worry about.

We'd have bomb drills at William Penn Elementary. These were similar to fire drills, but instead of going outside where we might be struck by shrapnel, we'd line up in single file and march down to the bomb shelters in the basement of the school. We were reassured that these were only practice sessions for the real thing, but either way it was a learning buzz kill. I mean, it was hard enough to learn cursive, or even basic arithmetic, when every time I heard a plane flying overhead I felt the urge to run to the basement with my hands covering the top of my head. Both Mrs. Anderson and Mrs. Jordan tried to act normal during the drills, like it was only a precaution in the most unlikely event the

Russians decided to drop the A-bomb on Salt Lake City. But we knew our teachers were antsy too.

We had to walk up the hill on Siggard Drive to our house after school. (We walked to school every day, *every single day*, whether it was snowing or not. Muggers? Snow drifts? Kidnappers? Child molesters? Ha! Try telling one of our parents that we shouldn't have had to walk five blocks to school during a rainstorm and let me know how that goes.) Planes would fly overhead on their daily runs from Los Angeles to Chicago and we'd watch them, looking skyward for the payload. When they'd pass by without dropping anything, we'd breathe a sigh of relief. Maybe they'd drop it on Des Moines or somewhere, but at least we'd dodged the bullet in Salt Lake City.

The Cold War seemed pretty hot to me. However, it hadn't been scripturally forecast so there remained the very real possibility that we might never get bombed at all. The same could not be said of the Second Coming. It was simply a matter of time before it happened. And you had to assume it was fast approaching because it couldn't stay nigh at hand forever, not with the world getting more wicked by the second, so the pressure for Jesus to get back here grew exponentially with each passing day.

The church taught us that Jesus would return to earth out of the clouds in all his glory. There would be heralding trumpets, and possibly harps. People would be looking up, shielding the glare with their hands, their mouths agape. And it was no secret where Jesus would show up. I hate to say it, but it wouldn't be Salt Lake City. No, he was scheduled to appear in Jackson County, Missouri.

Jesus would return to Jackson County, Missouri for the Second Coming because that's where the Garden of Eden had been located. This is something you probably haven't heard before, but Joseph Smith happened to come across the original Garden of Eden in Missouri while he was out taking a hike with some of the other church leaders. They were as surprised as anyone else because they'd all assumed the Garden of Eden would've been somewhere over near Egypt or somewhere.

Most Missourians don't even know about this. But it's true—Joseph found the original Garden of Eden in northwestern Missouri. In fact, he had the luck to come upon the very altar where Adam prayed and the exact spot where Cain killed Abel. So, if Jesus was going to return, which he definitely was, it only made sense that he would return to the original Garden of Eden.

It was forecast that when Jesus arrived, all the wicked people (basically we're talking about the Gentiles here) would be burnt crisp, wiped right off the face of the earth because of their wickedness unless they repented posthaste. I pictured the bewildered herd of unrepentant sinners scurrying for their lives, trying to hide from God's wrath. But I knew he'd find them, of course he would. And when he did, he'd smite them. Fortunately, we Saints would be spared because we belonged to the true church. It would be like well, whaddya know, look how the tables have turned! Look who's laughing now! All those church services I'd had to attend would finally pay off.

The good news was that we'd be saved due to our righteousness, but the bad news was that we might have to walk the entire way from Salt Lake City to Missouri because that's where we were supposed to gather once all the dust from the apocalypse settled. That would be the new Promised Land, right there next to the Garden of Eden. And I figured we'd probably have to walk because there wouldn't be enough gasoline to make it all the way there. Why no gas? Because of Armageddon.

My dad entertained us with lurid stories about the apocalypse, the ultimate day of reckoning, although he himself didn't seem the least bit worried about it, which surprised me a bit. In fact, I got the impression he even looked forward to it. I didn't, though. Don't get me wrong; I was happy we were the Chosen People and would dodge God's fury during the Second Coming, but walking all that way? I imagined us traipsing along, dog tired, zigzagging over dead Gentiles and the wreckage of burnt cars stranded along the interstate. We'd be hauling our sleeping bags and mason jars of canned peaches past the incinerated cathedrals, whorehouses, and synagogues, smoke still wafting up from them.

I don't think my mom bought into it like my dad did. He was the one who told us these harrowing tales, not my mom. In fact, I might have detected a slight eye roll on her part. Yeah, right, Leonard, like you know exactly how it's gonna be. Uh huh. If my mom had her druthers, I think she would've wanted Jesus's Second Coming to occur on Super Bowl Sunday, when all those heathens should've been in church. To be even more precise, she probably would've preferred that he come during the halftime show with all those "wardrobe malfunctions" and lascivious dancing.

In preparation for the Last Days (and there was zero doubt we were living in the Last Days) we stored food. Actually, we stored *a lot* of food, a cache of two years' worth to be exact. This was not a random time frame; it was a specific church commandment. All Mormons knew about the mandatory Two-Year Supply. Regrettably, we didn't buy tasty food—there were no Sugar Smacks for example. It was mostly dry wheat, rice, and cans of beans.

We dipped into our food storage from time to time. For example, there was a stretch of several years where all we drank was powdered milk and ate a lot of cracked wheat. At that point I didn't think I'd *want* to survive the apocalypse. I didn't wish to appear heathen, or the least bit unfaithful, but I pictured myself peeking out of the bomb shelter when the smoke cleared to see what wickedness had wrought. We'd climb out and then hunker down amongst the rubble of God's destructive wrath, looking like chimney sweepers with smudges of soot on our faces, passing around lukewarm cartons of powdered milk and gnawing on dry beef jerky.

When my mom died at the age of 75, we had to get rid of the 50-gallon drums of wheat stored on sturdy shelves in my parent's basement in order to sell the house. There was simply no way we could lift them, and the new owners (for some odd reason) didn't want to live in a house that had a bunker filled with 40-year-old drums of cracked wheat and survivalist supplies for the Last Days.

For the life of me, I don't know how my parents hoisted those 50-gallon drums down there in the first place. We finally resorted to punching a hole near the bottom of each drum with a screwdriver and allowing the wheat to pour out into gallon buckets, one bucket at a time. When a gallon bucket was full, one of my brothers would plug the hole in the drum like the Dutch boy with his finger in the dike, corking it, while another one of us put an empty gallon bucket below. This we did about 50 times until the damned things were finally empty. I imagined my parents looking down on us from heaven, horrified that we would be dumb enough to drain the very food source that would save our bacon during the apocalyptic Second Coming.

———————

Saturday nights were bath nights at our house, in preparation for Sunday. We were serious about keeping the Sabbath Day holy, so serious that we weren't allowed to do much on Sunday, hardly even bathe. (Now that I reflect on it, I think bathing would have been permitted, my parents just didn't want to do battle with us on Sunday morning). We were pretty skinny, all clavicles and hip bones, so more than one of us could fit in the tub, which saved a lot of time and water.

On Sunday morning we'd wake to Cream-o-Wheat which my dad would pour into a row of mismatched plastic cups directly from the pot and we'd drink it down. If my dad wasn't yet dressed for church, he'd likely be wearing my mom's powder blue bathrobe. We'd see her a half hour later, always smelling like perfume. Then we'd yank on our Sunday best and my mom would lick her palm and try to tamp down our cowlicks as we were herded into the station wagon for the two-block ride to the ward house.

A "ward" is a collection of about 500 Mormons, organized by neighborhoods. There are ward houses (or "churches" if you prefer) everywhere in Salt Lake City—probably one every few blocks. They are usually red-bricked with white steeples, the way I thought a church was supposed to look.

In Utah, "the church" could only mean the Mormon Church and there would be no need to clarify it. Utah isn't Rome. The wards are geographically bundled together to create a "stake". There are roughly 10 wards in each stake. I happened to grow up in the Valley View Tenth Ward along with most of my neighborhood buddies.

A visitor to Utah might be asked, "What ward are you in?" This question may sound presumptuous, but because there is still such a preponderance of Mormons in Utah, it's almost the standard greeting. That same visitor might stop to ask directions from a local, and because Mormons are so often kind and helpful, their reply might sound something like this: "Well, geez, let's see here. Okay, go down this street a few blocks until you see a ward on your left. Turn right and go another two blocks, then turn left at the stake house and you'll run into it." The poor Gentile will be driving around in circles looking for a steakhouse, and if he pulls over to ask someone else, he might be told, "Oh, that's over by Brother Jensen's place. Let's see, do you know where Bishop Rasmussen lives? No? Well, just go another few blocks and you can't miss it. It's right next to the stake house."

Anyway, on Sunday mornings my parents would load us into the station wagon. (This was before the advent of the minivan. Nowadays, 85% of the vehicles in a Mormon church parking lot are minivans.) There would always be a few stragglers who were stalling for one reason or another and there would be the usual dibs-ing (No, I called front!), teasing (Mom, Andy farted on me!), and complaining (Crud, why do we always have to go to stupid church).

Picture us unloading from the station wagon in the church parking lot, one at a time, all 12 of us, like those videos showing the number of people who can cram into a telephone booth. Now picture us walking through the corridor and past the huge mural depicting the time the seagulls were sent to save our ancestors from the cricket plague. From there we'd file into the chapel like the

Von Trapp family and then scoot sideways down the pew, taking the entire row. My parents and then all 10 blond towheads with our cowlicks and hair sticking up in spots, shirts mostly tucked in, some with belts, some not. Now picture the other ward members watching us file in. They'd tilt their heads and smile. Oh, what a perfectly large Mormon family, providing yet more credible evidence that we had a corner on the truth.

Of course, not all ward members felt the same way about our family, especially those with only two or three well-behaved children—the ones who hadn't received the memo about multiplying and replenishing the earth. Take Brother and Sister Cahoon, for example. They thought Leonard and Helen Driggs had gone off the rails, wildly out of control, obviously not fully comprehending how babies were made. And it couldn't have helped when 10 minutes into the service Paul was poking Dave, who was shooting a spit wad at Matt, while Steve was wiping a booger under the pew, and Danny was giving me a wet willy while I was patiently trying to play an innocent game of hangman. Picture my mom leaning over and looking down the row, finger to her lips, shushing us while my dad sat blithely oblivious to the chaos.

We weren't the only large family in the ward. Take the Sorensons, for example. They also had 10 kids, and so did the Youngs. There were several families with six or seven-plus kids. It seemed pretty normal to me, even fun. But I recall seeing a Monty Python movie when I was a teenager, and there was a scene where a Catholic woman was standing at the kitchen sink and babies were just dropping out of her, one at a time, like over-ripe fruit. I chuckled and thought to myself: What is up with those crazy Catholics and all the kids they have?

Church services on Sunday lasted three hours. This was fairly awful. Three hours? I suppose it was something to be endured by the adults too, even though many of them pretended to enjoy it. This pretense was a fraudulent display of Christian dishonesty. I mean, seriously, who among us would actually enjoy a three-hour church service? Even Jesus and Mary Magdalene would be squirming on the pew.

Mormons don't have a professional clergy. The leadership in each ward rotates every few years between the men in the neighborhood, along with all the other assignments in the ward (e.g. Sunday School teachers, choristers, and clerks). Nearly every adult in the ward has a church job, which Mormons refer to as "callings". That's why a Mormon wouldn't bat an eye if they ran into an old high school friend they hadn't seen for 20 years and the first thing the friend asked was: "So, Dale, what's your calling?"

Anyway, the bishop might be a plumber down the street for a few years and then the honor would switch to an accountant two streets over for the next few years. When I was a boy, our bishop happened to be a house painter. During Sunday services a man in the ward (usually not the bishop, who had his hands full with other things) would give a boring discourse on turning the other cheek, The Book of Mormon, or the joy of paying 10% tithing to the church. Often times, this sermon would be preceded by a youngster who'd been assigned to deliver a Two-And-A-Half-Minute-Talk. None of us actually *volunteered* for these talks.

The kids' talks were more interesting than the adults' talks—if not for the content, at least for the sheer amusement of seeing them up there at the pulpit, scared shitless, wearing an over-sized sport coat with a tie cinched so tight around their necks it looked like a noose, their parents in the congregation, beaming. Of course, they never lasted the full two-and-a-half minutes—they'd usually conk out after about a minute and a half. Two, tops. (It was like the times I'd been assigned a 500-word essay in school and I'd count each word, desperately trying to get to 500. If I was close, I'd throw in a bunch more "very's" to get me over the top. Thinking back on it now, I highly doubt my seventh-grade Social Studies teacher sat there hunched over my essay on Norway, counting the words.)

When I gave one of those talks in church it scared the crap out of me. My buddies were in the congregation undoubtedly pulling faces and threatening to shoot me with a spit wad, so it would've been deadly to look up because I'd start laughing. So I put my head down and read the damned thing. I recall the title of my talk was *Judge Not, Lest Ye Be Not Judged* (which is all we ever did). I said something about first taking the beam out of your own eye. I didn't know what it really meant, the whole beam thing, but I got it from my dad who said it came from the Bible, so I decided to go with it.

When the hour-long sacrament meeting finally ended, I'd walk down the hall from the chapel to my Sunday School classroom with my scuffed shoes and pants that hung well above my ankles. The pants would have previously been worn by Danny and would later be worn by Paul, Dave, and maybe Ben in a pinch. There were pictures on the wall of Joseph Smith and Jesus, both handsomely framed, side by side. The two men looked strikingly similar. Both had gorgeous golden-brown hair with blond highlights and big blue eyes. Jesus looked an awful lot like Fabio on the cover of a romance novel. It gave me no small comfort to know Jesus was also a Mormon.

In Sunday School we learned about the time that not only

Jesus but God himself visited Joseph Smith when he was only 14-years old, near his parent's farm in upstate New York. The details were a bit sketchy because Joseph didn't tell many people about it at the time (he wasn't sure they'd believe him). Later on, he reported that God and Jesus came down from heaven, together, and personally paid him a visit. The heavenly beings wore white flowing robes and hovered about a foot off the ground, just like Angel Moroni had. They didn't say much, only that the *true* church—the one Jesus established when he was on the earth—disappeared after all the original apostles had died off. This, regrettably, left nothing but a bunch of untrue churches scattered across the face of the earth. It was time to restore the true church, from scratch, and they wanted 14-year-old Joseph to head the effort. That's how the whole thing got started.

I'd been taught that this heavenly visit to Boy Joseph at the farm was the seminal moment in human history. Well, maybe not in the whole of human history, but at least in the last 2,000 years, ever since Jesus died on the cross and the true church went up in smoke. We could see God's patient hand, plodding along, setting the scene while mankind wandered in spiritual darkness since about 30 A.D., awaiting Joseph's triumphant restoration. Why was there a gap of 1,800 years without a true church on earth? I wasn't sure, but I figured there was a perfectly valid reason. Besides, it must have taken a while to set it all up—God couldn't just do it overnight because these things took time, the pieces had to be set in motion.

When peering through history, it was easy to see the preparation taking shape too, especially with the benefit of hindsight. I noticed how God strategically waited for the printing press to be invented. And how he waited until there was a country with religious freedom, one that had a good constitution. That's why he inspired the Founding Fathers to write it the way they did in the first place, so that 50 years later Joseph could restore the true church in a land without religious oppression. See what I mean?

Once Joseph finished The Book of Mormon, he decided the Bible also needed a little touching up. Mormons believe the Bible is the word of God, but only to the extent that it has been translated correctly. And because Joseph now had experience translating ancient tomes, he figured he ought to take a crack at the Bible too—just to be sure it was as accurate as it could possibly be, even though most Gentiles figured the Bible was the Bible and didn't need to be tinkered with.

When Joseph began his final-of-final edit of the Bible, he started with what he titled The Book of Moses, which should have been included from the get-go but wasn't for some reason. But perhaps the greatest discovery of Joseph's Bible was a newly edited passage in Genesis which actually predicted that he, Joseph, would come along in the Last Days to restore the true church. Here's Joseph's edited Biblical prophecy from 1830, word for word, and then you tell my younger self that Mormons didn't have the truth: "A seer would arise in the latter days and would be called Joseph, after the name of his father." This seer would be "highly esteemed and would be great like unto Moses." Joseph Smith's father was also named Joseph, so we were all hard-pressed to figure out who *else* the Bible would've been referring to. It seemed pretty obvious, wouldn't you think? This particular passage must have been edited out centuries earlier, so Joseph stuck it back in where it should've stayed all along.

We could see that God was a careful planner, setting the stage for Joseph to come along and restore his true church. Unfortunately, Satan also happened to be a patient planner. He was a schemer and was very good at what he did, too. He could make something bad look good. Knowing that, I was always a bit off balance, wondering if Satan was lurking in the shadows, up to his dirty tricks, making me think that something bad, like, say, lusting after Debbie Ludlow, was actually a good thing.

If we were lucky, we'd get to see a movie during Sunday School. It might not be *Mary Poppins* but it would still be a diversion from a boring regular lesson on something like faith. One movie I practically had memorized was the short Mormon film titled *Johnny Lingo*.

Johnny was a trader who lived on a Polynesian island. He really liked an ugly girl and wanted to marry her. All his neighbors thought this was hilarious. "You want to marry *her?* Are you freaking blind?" But Johnny wouldn't be dissuaded. All the other haughty women on the island bragged about how many cows their husbands had given up to snag them. "My husband paid three cows for me!"

The ugly girl's father demanded three cows for her and people snickered. For her? No way. They figured Johnny would counter with one cow, and an old one at that. But he didn't. He said that three cows were indeed a lot, but not enough for his girl. He then offered the unheard-of price of eight cows for her hand in marriage. Eight cows? For *her?* Was he insane? Sure enough, Johnny gave the cows and took his bride. When they returned from their honeymoon, all the townspeople were astonished to see that the girl had gone from ugly to hot, for Johnny had proven to her that her true worth had nothing to do with what others saw. I thought this was a nice story, but I wondered how the film makers could make her look so homely during most of the film and then so beautiful at the end.

If we'd seen *Johnny Lingo* too many times, we'd be treated to stories of the Bible's greatest hits. There'd be the one about poor Daniel who was hauled off to the lion's den. And do you remember why? For praying in public, that's why. Where was the constitution when you needed it? But God turned him into the Lion Whisperer and the hungry lions only purred and licked. Or how about the story of David and Goliath, that nine-foot tall giant who was as mean as they get? I can still picture David with his tunic and sandals, armed with nothing but a flimsy slingshot. Now he's twirling it around and around his head like a lariat before letting the rock fly straight into Goliath's head. *Thunk!* Got him right between the eyes.

There were other stories too, like the one about Samson and how he beat the crap out of all the bad guys after they'd cut his hair and gouged his eyes out. But my favorite might have been the story of Jonah who was swallowed by the whale. I pictured him sitting before a small campfire in the belly of that damned whale. He'd be holding a stick with a smaller fish impaled on it, slowly waving it back and forth over the fire like he was cooking s'mores, wondering if he'd ever get out of that jam alive.

And for sheer gore, I liked the one about John the Baptist. He'd called out the mother of a spoiled rotten tramp named Salome for sleeping with her brother-in-law. This tramp, Salome, danced seductively in front of King Herod to get on his good side. The king was so turned on he asked her what she wanted. She demanded John the Baptist's head on a silver platter. The king obliged and I could picture in my mind John's hairy head sitting upright on the platter, like a rump roast surrounded by a marinade of blood. It was all very inspiring and it made us want to be good Mormons.

After church my dad would take a nap on the shag carpet in

the living room, surrounded by the newspaper funnies and all the chaos. Because it was Sunday, there was only so much we could do without violating the Sabbath Day rule. It would have been lovely if we'd all sat around trying to hog the Bible for some light reading, or if we'd visited the sick with a tuna noodle casserole, things that were tailor-made for Sunday. But instead we played Monopoly or Sorry and sometimes we played cards (but not face cards).

We gallantly tried to find something to do that wouldn't offend God on his special day. This we navigated through trial and error, eventually realizing we *were* allowed to shoot basketballs in the driveway but we *weren't* allowed to walk down to the tennis court to hit balls because that would be a violation of the Sabbath Day. We *could* run in the sprinklers, maybe even do the Slip n' Slide, but we *couldn't* actually go swimming. It was resolved that getting a kick-the-can game together was permissible, provided it was impromptu and not formally planned.

The only flagrant violation of keeping the Sabbath Day holy occurred when I was a teenager. Danny and I were helping my dad build an addition to his office building. (We'd barely even built a tree hut and didn't know what we were doing.) We poured the concrete on a Saturday. The forms had to be removed the following day or else they'd be stuck to the concrete permanently. Of course, this was a no-brainer violation of the commandment, working on a Sunday, but that one time we did it anyway. Several months later when the construction project was completed, the floor dipped about two inches at the junction of the addition because I'd measured wrong. My dad was cool about it. All he said was, "I don't think anyone will even notice. You've done a great job—you're one of the best carpenters I've ever seen."

5

I HAD MY FIRST CRUSH IN THE second grade. I sat by Debbie Ludlow and finally mustered the courage to speak to her. What followed can only be described as a whirlwind five-day romance that culminated in a gift to her of my prized geode (half of it, anyway). The next day we were doing multiplication tables when I had the urge to pee. I thought I could outlast it, at first. But within 20 minutes it was bad. I asked Mrs. Harrow if I could use the bathroom but she denied me and sent me back to my desk, assuring me that I would be fine when I knew I wouldn't. She said the lunch hour was only 15 minutes away. Just hold it, she said. I squirmed and concentrated on anything else until finally it was no use. I peed my pants.

I'd only meant to let a little leak out, just enough to take the pressure off, maybe a pint. But once I started, it felt so good I couldn't stop. It was so warm and felt heavenly for a few seconds before it got cold. The damned bell rang just as it was getting cold and I realized the enormity of my mistake. I stood up as all the other kids were leaving the room to see a small puddle on my chair.

Mike Baxter saw my wet pants and made sure everyone else saw them too, pointing at me with a mixture of hilarity and condemnation. The girls squealed. Eww, how gross! And then I saw her, huddled with Laura Tillotson and Becky Farnsworth, pointing at me with that disgusting look on her face, like she'd never peed the bed in her life. Debbie never spoke to me again. Not one word. She didn't even give my geode back to me.

I walked home, alone, after school. (My mom come and get me? Are you kidding? We walked, remember?) My pants were almost dry by the time I made it home but there remained the outline of my shame, a semi-circle of regret nearly to my knees. As soon as I walked in the door I started to cry.

My mom was good in a crisis. You can ask any of my siblings. She always knew the right thing to say, or not say. Take the time my little sister, Jane, was distraught after breaking up with her 16-year-old boyfriend. My mom made an elaborate show of taking a glass of orange juice to her on a TV tray. The glass rested on a fancy doily and everything. My mom told her the juice had poison in it, in case the pain became too great.

Anyway, my mom told me I'd be fine and peeing your pants wasn't that big of a deal. In fact, she said 90-year-old Brother Harding down the street did it all the time. Besides, she and my dad had a fun surprise to tell us about that night. Great, another kid in the oven, I thought. That's all we needed. But it wasn't that. We were going to Disneyland! I think my parents were as excited as we were.

It was a midnight in early June when we piled into the car that had all our luggage lashed to the top. My dad wanted to leave at midnight because we didn't have air conditioning and it was a 12-hour drive. He laid the seats down in the back of the station wagon and we put in as many pillows and blankets as would fit. Then we laid down in the back, sausage style. My dad was behind the wheel, my mom was in the passenger seat with Ben on her lap, and Matt was on the floor by her feet. The rest of us were like mummies in the back, too excited to complain that we were being breathed upon or that somebody wiggled, or farted.

We rolled into Vegas at about seven o'clock in the morning like the Beverly Hillbillies. My dad made some adjustments to the luggage straps on top that had been flapping all night and then we had breakfast at a little café next to the Golden Nugget. When we got back in the car my dad was missing. We asked mom where he'd gone and she only grunted. What could this mean? It was hot in the car as we waited in the early Las Vegas sun, my mom furious but trying to hide it while the rest of us wondered where our dad could be. Twenty minutes later, we saw him bounding across the parking lot, a huge smile as he approached (my dad was always in a good mood). He winked and gave my mom a kiss as she turned her head away from him. Oh boy. We finally divined that he'd left us for "a few minutes" to finance our trip at the craps table. I'm pretty sure he won some money, but we never knew because he would have been happy either way. I think my mom would have been mad about gambling even if he'd won the million-dollar jackpot.

The drive through the Mojave Desert was rugged with no air conditioning and everybody breathing. And it's tough to play the alphabet game when there aren't any billboards. We rolled down the windows and were blasted by scorching air, but at least it was moving. Then the fan belt broke and we waited on the side of the road, sweating, until my dad could fix it (my dad could fix anything with a screwdriver, or a wad of gum). We stopped for a milk shake in Baker right next to the world's tallest thermometer. This trip was amazing! My dad put his milk shake on the dashboard so it could roast in the sun for about an hour and then he drank it.

The best thing about our trip to Disneyland was that we were staying at a motel in Anaheim with a heated swimming pool and a *TV!* We didn't have a television growing up. My parents said we couldn't afford one, and that might have been true, but the more I think about it, I believe it was because my mom thought television would corrupt us. I only say that because the Pierces had one and they seemed a lot poorer than we did. (About five years later, we rented an old black and white job with aluminum foil on the rabbit ears to watch the moon landing. It was the summer of 1969 and I was 13. We set it up on the planter box outside our front door and ran an extension cord into the house. Then we all sat on our front lawn and watched in awe as mankind made that giant leap.)

Did I miss much because I wasn't able to gorge on episodes of *Gilligan's Island* and *Petticoat Junction?* Was my childhood robbed, my development retarded? These questions have only academic poignancy now because what's done is done. (*Spoiler Alert!* They made if off the island when the Professor accurately predicted a tsunami and they built a homemade raft, something I never saw coming.)

But when I was in the second grade, we still didn't have a TV, so the motel in Anaheim was a real treat. We'd rented one room with two queen beds, so it was about as roomy as the back of the station wagon. Disneyland, on the other hand, was amazing. We couldn't afford to buy any food there (my mom packed in baloney sandwiches) and I watched other patrons feasting on frozen bananas, fudgsicles, and hamburgers that cost almost $2.00. My mouth salivated. Who were these lucky zillionaires? Were they Walt's relatives? I swore that one day when I was old I would return to Disneyland and buy a hamburger. (Many years later I did return, but by then the burgers were $12.00 and there was no way I was going to be suckered into spending that kind of money on a hamburger, so I didn't, purely out of principle.)

Disneyland was heaven, at least for the first few hours. We were all in Frontierland, shooting at the ducks in a barrel, when I turned around and realized my family was missing. I felt no panic at first. I figured they were just around the corner at the Tiki Hut. But no, they weren't there either. I roamed for about an hour with no luck when, finally, a kind Disneyland employee saw me crying, obviously lost. She took me to the Lost and Found across from Main Street where the animated Abraham Lincoln exhibit was. Of course, I had no ID and cell phones were still almost 40 years away. I waited there for two more hours, until finally I saw my dad coming down Main Street heading straight for the Lost and Found.

My family had left the park hours earlier and returned to the motel a few miles away where my brothers and sisters were having the time of their lives, swimming and watching color TV. I guess it was only then that they counted heads, and then counted them again. Someone was missing! It's 7-year-old Warren. Hey, anybody seen Warren? Where's Warren? My dad hightailed it back to Disneyland to track me down.

On the way out, my dad bought me a fudgsicle which I knew was his way of saying he was sorry (and he said it about 10 times). I loved my dad for all I was worth so it was easy to forgive him. We returned back to the motel and I went swimming, as content as I could be. No one said a thing.

———

It was shortly after we returned from Anaheim that Danny and I made a fire with flint and steel wool in eight seconds. You heard that right: My 8-year-old older brother and I started a fire, with plenty of witnesses and a stop watch, using only a piece of flint and steel wool in eight seconds. We did it while at a Boy Scout function (our dad was the scoutmaster and he took us along where we showed up all the older boys and the adults too). My Grandma Driggs sewed a pennant to commemorate the proud achievement. I still have it. It's made of green felt and sewn across the pennant the red-velvet letters read: "Daniel & Warren made fire by friction in eight sec." This may not have been the highwater mark of my life, but *eight seconds?* Seriously? Let's see you do it. I don't know how we did it and I'm confident that if I were forced to make a fire now without matches and lighter fluid I'd probably starve or freeze to death.

If only Debbie Ludlow could've seen that pennant she'd have to live the rest of her life with the weighty regret over the kind of man she let get away. Barring that, I simply hope she's fat.

––––––––––

Because I idolized my dad, I was devasted the only time he got mad at me. It was probably the same summer as Disneyland and we were camping in the mountains just east of Salt Lake City. There were a number of squirrels in our camp and I was throwing rocks at them. My aim wasn't very good, but I managed to hit one. It lay squirming on the ground, not quite dead, so I hit it again.

My dad came upon the scene and flipped out. It caught me off guard. My mild-mannered dad, always happy, always my greatest fan, was furious. How could I have done such a thing? And why?

It was cruel and that wasn't like me, he said. What could I say? What was my defense? The evidence of my cruelty lay before me in the dust next to a few fallen pine cones. I would have taken it all back, I would have become lost again at Disneyland, this time for twice as long, not to have disappointed my dad so much.

Why had I intentionally killed that squirrel? For sport? They say serial killers intentionally harm animals when they are children, as if they have no conscience or perhaps enjoy seeing a living thing suffer. But I was not a sociopath. I believe I had empathy. At no time did I seriously consider myself a threat to humanity. At no time did I feel the urge to stab someone. And neither did I get a particular rush over this cruelty. So why had I done it? I was somehow disconnected from this squirrel's suffering.

My dad had never laid a hand on me, and he didn't do it then. But I wished he had. I wished he had spanked me or grabbed my skinny arm and squeezed too hard. But he didn't. His disapproval was plenty and it made a mark on me like a welt could never do.

My friends and I also caught a few grasshoppers and experimented trying to fry them with a magnifying glass out on the cement driveway. Did this make me a budding sociopath? Would a child psychologist have raised the alarm? Hey, keep an eye on that kid? Perhaps.

Notwithstanding the disapproval from my dad over the dead squirrel, I couldn't help but recall that six months earlier he'd taken Danny and me deer hunting. He hadn't shot any deer, but he'd tried. Why, I wondered, was it okay to shoot a deer but not stone a squirrel? For that matter, it got me thinking about the mouse trap we had in the kitchen, and the glee we all felt, even my dad, when we heard the *snap!* I stepped on ants and spiders and we had a fly swatter on a hook just inside the pantry door hanging next to the collection of my mom's homemade aprons. I ultimately decided this was too heavy to contemplate. And if I *had* contemplated it? Could I have then, or even now, articulated an appreciable difference between a deer, a squirrel, and a spider? If there was no justifiable basis for stoning an innocent squirrel, where was the justification for the rat bait out behind the shed in the backyard?

Several years after the squirrel-killing episode, I went deer hunting with some friends. I was 18. I was sitting on a rock in the middle of a pine forest a few hundred yards above a lovely meadow, swatting at bugs on my neck. Suddenly, a large buck came meandering through the meadow. It was the most magnificent thing I had ever seen. It turned up the meadow and started walking directly toward me. My gun was resting on my lap. I froze as the deer approached, oblivious to its fate. When the deer was about 20 feet away from me, it saw me and it froze too, staring at me with a look in its eye. It's a look that still haunts me. It's a look that said "Please don't do this."

I didn't even lift the gun to my shoulder. Instead I held it waist high and fired. The buck looked at me, cocked its head with a look of helplessness and pity for me. Pity for me, I imagined, that I would be so cruel, that I would shoot it for no reason other than I could. Then it buckled to its front knees and collapsed right in front of me, its eyes still open.

I was horrified at what I'd done. It was so intimate, this killing. My friends heard the shot and came running, excited—ecstatic really—for it was a magnificent trophy.

I dropped the gun and haven't shot one since.

6

MY BROTHER DANNY HAS BEEN MY BEST friend for 60 years. Let's make that about 52, because the first several years were rough (and I have the scars to prove it). He has always been as loyal as a hound to me—always protected me and had my back. I first realized this devotion in the third grade.

Our elementary school was on Siggard Drive, a road that has an extremely steep hill (at least it seemed that way when we had to walk home every single day). There was a convenience store at the bottom of the hill, maybe a block and a half farther down from the school. The store was called Wimmers. Danny was in the fourth grade and was a rebel. He talked me into ditching school during the lunch recess and sneaking off down the hill to drink a Coke at Wimmers. This adventure was fraught with double jeopardy. First of all, we'd be leaving the school grounds which was an obvious no-no. Not only that, but we'd be committing one no-no in order to commit another one: drink Coke. Coca-Cola had caffeine and was against the commandments. This, I knew, was wicked. Danny knew it too, but he acted like he didn't care.

We escaped the playground unseen and walked down the hill, on the lam. I glanced over my shoulder every few steps, looking for the cops. We drank a Coke at Wimmers and played a game of pinball, things only hoods would do. Then we trudged back up the hill, hoping to return before the bell rang. We were on the sidewalk adjacent to the playground, separated only by a chain link fence, when Jill Rasmussen saw us. If there's one thing we knew about Jill Rasmussen it was that she was a snitch.

I walked into my third-grade class and sat at my desk, harboring the guilt of our crime but satisfied that we had pulled it off. Five minutes later I looked up to see Danny walk into my classroom and approach Mrs. Robertson. He handed her a folded-up note. Mrs. Robertson read it and then frowned. Uh oh. She called me up to the front and then escorted both of us to the principal's office. I remember walking forlornly a few paces behind her and wondering how she fit into her dress. It looked like she'd been poured into it and forgot to say 'when'. It's funny what you think about at a time like that, a time when I should have been composing a heartfelt confession.

You see, Danny had learned to write in cursive and assumed that cursive was cursive was cursive. He also assumed Jill Rasmussen was a rat. Therefore, he did the most sensible thing he could think of to save me: he forged a note from our mom.

Dear Mrs. Robertsen [sic]. *Warren has permision* [sic] *to go to Wimmers during lunch to drink Coke if he wants to. Signed* (with a flourish), *Mrs. Driggs.*

We were both sent home, presumably to face the everlasting wrath of our parents. The hill seemed even steeper as we contemplated our fate, heads down, kicking at rocks as we went. We had been expelled and only hoods got expelled, so this was uncharted territory. I wasn't mad at Danny. In fact, I loved him for what he'd done and I wanted to think I would've done the same thing for him. But I knew my cursive was still too unrefined and, truthfully, I probably would have chickened out. But Danny had no cowardice at all and I respected him for it.

I remember walking into the house like up the steps to the gallows. My mom asked for the note and read it. She knew how to read cursive so we studied her face. She didn't even seem that mad, or maybe it was just our wishful thinking. She said we'd talk about it when our dad came home. Danny and I went downstairs, to the fruit room (that's what we called our food storage room with all the cans of wheat and creamed corn) and found a stack of old National Geographics (we'd previously scoured them looking for photo spreads of topless African women). We shoved two each down our pants to cover our butts, hoping it'd provide some cushioning. I had never been spanked in my life, but I'd heard about it and knew it wasn't pretty.

My dad came down to see us after he returned home from work. We braced. But my dad wasn't mad. Oh, he pretended to be a little upset I suppose, for show. But it occurred to me that he was...what? Proud? Amused? Impressed with our loyalty and friendship? He asked us if we wanted one big one or 10 small ones. I chose to get it over with and picked one big one. I leaned over his knee and he gave me the softest big one there could possibly be. It didn't even hurt. He then stood me up so I was face to face with him as he sat on a five-gallon bucket of cracked wheat. He held me by the shoulders and looked me dead in the eye. "I love you son. And I am proud of you. Now be a good boy."

I never wanted to disappoint my dad again.

But I'm sure I did, because I was only 8 and had a long life ahead of me.

———————

Shortly after the school-ditching-Coke-guzzling crime spree, I overheard my mom talking on the phone to my aunt Eloise. My aunt was telling her that my cousins had the chicken pox. "Oh, that's awful," my mom was saying. "I know how catchy they are. I think I'll send Danny, Warren, Jane, and Paul over to your place this afternoon if you don't mind. They might as well catch them now, don't you think?"

Huh? My mom was sacrificing me to a lethal dose of chicken pox? On purpose? Really mom? You *want* me to contract a near fatal illness? Is this because of Wimmers? I was stunned. But there she was, my own mother, sending me to the wolves.

When we arrived, I saw my speckled, miserable cousins laying on the floor playing with Lincoln logs. Obviously, I didn't want to get anywhere near them, but my aunt made me get right down there on the floor with them to build a log cabin. I couldn't believe it was happening.

A few days later the itching began.

———————

It was a few months later that Danny and I started the house on fire. We had a nice little Christmas manger scene on the mantle of the fireplace. Actually, now that I think back on it, it was a white Christmas scene with a little house in the woods combined with a traditional manger scene with a three-sided barn. This is the only time I've seen Frosty the Snowman at Jesus's birth. To make it seem more authentic, my mom had dolled it up with some of that white fiberglass "snow". It turned out that stuff was flammable.

We'd pull a string of snow, like the thread of a spider web, and light the end. The fire would race up the string but die out before reaching the snow. Well, except for the last time. That last time, the snow covering the whole fireplace mantle was on fire within seconds. We were petrified and started screaming. The next thing I knew, our neighbor, Ellery Hansen, was leaping over our grape stake fence. First, he grabbed a sleeping bag and tried to smother it but that just made it worse. Then he dragged a hose into our house and started squirting. I couldn't believe it—he was squirting the garden hose *inside* the house. When the smoke cleared, the wall above the mantle was black and small stalactites of water hung from the ceiling. The floor was covered with water. All that was left of the manger were a few blackened farm animals, a melted snowman, and the charred remains of a wise man. Baby Jesus had been reduced to a little black ball.

I don't remember my parents getting mad at us for that. Maybe they'd been so relieved the house hadn't burned to the ground that they completely forgot to administer fair punishment. I knew they couldn't have been *that* mad because once a year one of us older children got to go Christmas shopping for Santa Claus with my dad. That was my year and I was allowed to do it in spite of the fire. I'd just (finally) learned that Santa was actually my dad. And because he didn't have a toy factory, he had to go buy everything, and he'd usually do it all at once. A few days before Christmas, my dad and I climbed into the station wagon to go buy stuff for Santa Claus. I was sworn to secrecy. I'll never forget walking down the aisles of

Kmart chasing the blue light specials. I threw whatever struck my fancy into the cart. Paul might like this. Ben might like that. And, oh, I *know* Matt would love this. What fun!

It'd been a slight bummer to learn that Santa Claus wasn't real—that it had all been a gigantic lie. But at the same time, it was somehow reassuring to know that I didn't have to rely on Santa 100% of the time, because there was always the lurking knowledge that he'd know if I'd been naughty.

There were definite corollaries between Santa Claus and God. Both had magical powers. Both had white beards. Both could fly. Both were generally nice (although they were known to carry a grudge at times). And both were judging my behavior in real time—they knew darned well what I'd done in the privacy of my bedroom, and could even peer into my darker thoughts. Therefore, I was staring down the very real possibility that I'd get a lump of coal in the short run and everlasting hell in the long run (I generally focused more on the short run, so short-sighted was I). So, yes, once I learned Santa wasn't real, there was some relief in knowing that, at least during Christmas time, there would be no direct cause-and-effect relationship to my sinning.

Since Santa Claus didn't wrap the gifts at our house, we lined up at five o'clock on Christmas morning and walked into the living room to all that loot. I recognized everything except the microscope and Johnny Cash album that Santa had left for me on the arm of the sofa next to my Christmas stocking filled with a Pez dispenser, large Hershey bar, and an orange in the toe. I didn't know what prompted Santa to believe I would enjoy a Johnny Cash album.

My siblings were so dumb. They didn't even know that I had been Santa's helper. I sent a self-satisfied look across the room to my dad who was trying to get the eight-millimeter movie camera going, the kind that required a separate piece of equipment with four bazillion-watt light bulbs to illuminate the scene. There is still footage from that morning of my siblings holding up their new pair of jammies or Tonka truck up to the light, eyes squinting, while my dad filmed away.

———

Next to Christmas, July 24th is the biggest holiday in Utah. That's the 24th, not the 4th. You see, July 24, 1847 was the day Brigham Young and the first band of Mormons rolled into the Salt Lake Valley, dog-tired from their long trek. It's the state holiday. I don't recall if Salt Lake City had a parade on the 4th but we sure had a big one on the 24th. It ran all the way down State Street, past Sears and then east to Liberty Park. We were proud that it was one of the biggest parades in the country! (It might have recently been eclipsed by the Gay Pride parade that Salt Lake has now, a flamboyant affair that would cause poor Brigham to roll over in his grave.)

We once camped out along the route the night before the parade to secure a good spot to see the floats—right there on the sidewalk with our quilts, folding lawn chairs, and Coleman cooler. There were other campers nearby and one of them said the F word. My mom told my dad to tell the guy to knock it off. I could tell my dad didn't really want to because he didn't think it warranted a scene. So my mom was mad at the guy who swore *and* at my dad, as if he had aided and abetted this wholesale wickedness. After all, we knew that evil prevailed when good men did nothing. In fact, because my dad wouldn't stand up to sin in the moment, I think she was more upset at him than the sailor.

"Well, Leonard, if you won't say something, then I will!" She marched up to the guy and gave him a tongue lashing. Personally, I thought she overdid it a bit. When she had finished and walked away, I saw the guy turn to his buddies and start snickering. I wanted to swear at him.

7

I WAS A MEDIOCRE STUDENT. I CAN'T blame my teachers for that (even though I thought Mrs. Harrow was an awful woman). I think my intellect was consistent with my average grades. This childhood mediocrity was uncommented upon, except perhaps by my dad who thought I was a Sterling Scholar even though he didn't have a clue what my grades were like. In fact, he didn't even know what grade I was in (my mom probably knew, but that's not a certainty). "Let's see now, Julie would be in the, what, fifth grade? So, I guess that'd put Danny in the fourth and Warren in the third. Yeah, I think that sounds about right."

I never thought my parents cared much about school. My mom had dropped out of high school after the 11th grade to get married and my dad had graduated by the skin of his teeth. (For the record, my parents didn't rush to the altar because my mom was pregnant. At least I don't think she was. I presume she just decided she didn't want to go to the high school sock hop as a married woman.) The possibility of college was hardly spoken of. To the extent it came up, there was a general bias against it, as if a college education came part and parcel with an ugly hedonistic arrogance. Intellectualism was not a virtue in my community, or at least not in my house. Intellectuals were the ones on their high horses who looked down their snobby noses at those of us who had a wary suspicion of evolution. We Mormons believed in strict creationism, not evolution. We're not monkeys, my church leaders said. So-called modern science and snooty intellectuals with their weak-kneed capitulation to Satan would not do. After high school it was taken for granted that I would go on a Mormon mission, get married, have a passel of my own children, and pay tithing to the church. And that would be that.

I entered the third-grade spelling bee. Unfortunately, I conked out in the second round when I couldn't spell the word "vacuum" contrary to the assurance of my dad, who said I would probably win the whole enchilada. Of course, this assurance coming from my dad shouldn't have carried the same weight as if it'd come from, say, Einstein, because my dad was so irrationally exuberant about my talents. Besides that, my dad was the worst speller I knew. I still have my birthday card where he spelled my name "Woran". Happy Birthday Woran! Really dad? You can't spell my *name?* And how about the time my little sister, Jane, sang in her high school's concert choir? The fee was $15.00 and my dad wrote the check payable to The Quonsert Quire.

So, yeah, I was no genius and I think it was genetic. As an adult, I rifled through my old report cards from grade school to confirm what I thought to be true. Sure enough, I was an average student who got along well with his peers. I had pretty much given up on academics by the time I reached high school. If my parents didn't care, then why should I? If they ever asked about my grades (which they never did) I'd just lie anyway. So they didn't know I earned a 1.5 GPA my senior year. Of course, that might have been because I was expelled for much of it. (I'll tell you that story later.) This poor performance in school is not something I'm particularly proud of because, really, how hard is it when the teachers are just trying to herd you through the system? It is something of a permanent regret that I couldn't get at least a few A's.

Notwithstanding my dad's learning disabilities, and the fact that I was always haunted by math, Utah has the highest literacy rate in America. I'm not a social scientist, and I don't know the criteria for ranking such things, but this stellar literacy in Utah might have something to do with a devotion to elementary education, or perhaps a lack of inner-city poverty (Utah has it, of course, but I suspect Utah has a relatively even socio-economic keel in comparison to other worldly places). Maybe it's the high percentage of intact nuclear families, or the cultural and welfare safety net of the church. Or, come to think of it, maybe it's all the scripture reading. After all, anyone who can plow through The Book of Mormon should be able to breeze right through Herman Melville or James Fenimore Cooper. Anyone but me, anyway.

So, while I may have bucked the literacy trend in Utah, I never lacked for self-esteem, even in the face of my mediocrity. I always assumed I'd be successful without any rational basis whatsoever. Where did this optimism come from in a boy who couldn't even subtract if he had to carry? This naïve confidence, I believe, was the singular result of my dad's enthusiasm over my modest talents. Therefore, it didn't send me into therapy when Mrs. Harrow called me out in the second grade for being such an idiot.

The school administrators at William Penn Elementary had two oil paintings and they were trying to decide which of the two should be hung in the main foyer of the school. One painting was that of a mountain landscape and the other was of a young girl sitting on a chair surrounded by sunflowers. They decided to allow the students to vote, which now seems like a smart idea coming from a school administrator.

The paintings were taken to each classroom and displayed at the front. Mrs. Harrow then informed us that the landscape painting was much better. Personally, I thought they were both lovely. A secret ballot was then passed around to each of us for the big vote. When the votes were tabulated, the landscape won handily—28 votes to 1.

Mrs. Harrow was upset. Who, she demanded to know, was the numbskull who'd voted for the painting of the girl and the sunflowers? I very reluctantly raised my hand because I was not a naturally born anarchist. She proceeded to tell the class that I was the only one, *the only one*, who'd voted for that dumb painting. I was so red in the face I'm sure it looked like I'd come down with a fever. Yes, Mrs. Harrow was an awful woman. And a terrible teacher. If I had to do it over, I would have voted for the girl again, not out of spite, but because I liked it the best (and, truthfully, maybe out of a little bit of spite).

And if I had to do it over again, I would have also stuck with "ant." Mrs. Harrow asked us all what kind of animal we'd be if we could choose. This seemed to be a fair question and I thought being an ant was a fair answer. But she didn't. An *ant?* She looked around the room at the other students. Warren would like to be an ant. Well, it was true. Ants get along well with others, they are industrious, and they have super-human strength. I'd like to have seen Mrs. Harrow lift something 5,000 times her own weight and haul it around like it was nothing. Why didn't she tell Susan Moffatt she was an idiot for wanting to be a robin? Who would want to be a robin? I just think she had it out for me.

I remember all the teachers were upset the day JFK was shot. We were cutting out accordion-fan turkeys when the principal made the announcement over the intercom. Mrs. Harrow put her head on her desk and cried. Geez, this had to be bad. I thought she must have personally known him because she was crying so hard. I'd heard of President Kennedy and could have picked his photo out of a line-up, but it wasn't like I had been on his campaign staff or anything. I was only in the third grade. They let us out of school early that day. I don't remember my parents being that upset about it, probably because he was a Democrat. But that is unfair because I just don't remember.

I went over to Steve's house, my buddy across the street. Their TV was on and Steve's mom was glued to it. She was sad, more so than my mom. Maybe that's because my mom didn't have a TV and was busy doing other things. I wondered why Steve's mom kept watching something that made her so sad, but it seemed to me like she almost wanted to feel that way. I remember the funeral procession with Kennedy's flag-draped casket on a wagon with large spoked wheels being pulled by a rider-less horse and I wondered why they didn't just put it in the back of a station wagon. I even remember his little son and daughter, and the salute.

These memories are very real, but it makes me wonder if they rely, at least partially, on the fact that I've seen images of that tragedy many times over the decades. Is that why I remember them so well? Has my memory been tricked, aided? Perhaps so, which causes me to have more faith in memories that were not recorded by Polaroid. In my particular case, that is fairly easy because there are not more than 10 to 15 photos of me between my birth and the time I was in school, and those are group photos, at that.

8

I SPENT A LOT OF TIME OVER at Steve's. We played catch in his backyard for hours at a time, throwing pop-ups and grounders, just like Mickey Mantle would do. When we'd miss the ball, it would roll into the petunias and we'd go in after it, trampling them down without a thought. Steve's mom didn't even get mad.

She was pretty, with bleached platinum-blond hair, and seemed to be interested in fashion. She didn't wear a muumuu every day like my mom did. I remember her sunbathing in their backyard. She'd put a blanket down in the middle of the grass and then a few strips of tin foil on top of that. She rubbed herself down with oil and lay on her stomach in a two-piece bathing suit (a bikini!) next to a plastic oven timer. We threw the ball over her, for hours at a time. I remember thinking she was the most exotic thing I had ever seen. The thought of my mom sunbathing, and in a two-piece no less, was unthinkable.

I worried about Steve's mom because I'd seen her drink coffee (even though she was supposed to be a Mormon). The Mormon Word of Wisdom specifically forbade alcohol, tobacco, and coffee. The Word of Wisdom was a litmus test for righteousness with little margin for error. The bottom line was this: Our bodies are temples and we shouldn't defile them with a Marlborough, Bud Light, or cup of Folgers. It was pretty easy to see who was going to heaven and who was headed for the brimstone—all you had to do was look in their pantry. You didn't even need to go that far if they had a Mr. Coffee on their kitchen counter in plain sight.

In my small little world, it was impossible to differentiate levels of sin. Sin was sin. Drinking a beer was equivalent to robbing a bank, and smoking a cigarette ranked right up there with taking the Lord's name in vain. I figured you were doomed for eternity either way and it made absolutely no sense to complicate things with a life of unbridled sin. Why take a straight line to heaven and make it crooked?

I recall seeing parents at Liberty Park who were chasing their kids around. The dad was smoking a cigarette and I had such overwhelming pity for those children because I assumed their dad must have been a terrible person. And if he was a terrible person, it only stood to reason that he was an awful father who didn't love his children. I was able to quickly deduce all this because he was smoking. I watched him push his kids on the swing, wondering when he might push them too far, something a wicked person would do.

The discovery of this additional barometer to measure wickedness occurred in 1833 when God personally dictated the Word of Wisdom to Joseph Smith, word for word. No alcohol, tobacco, coffee, or tea. Period. This wasn't something to toy around with. You couldn't go to the Celestial Kingdom if you broke the Word of Wisdom. (I should explain about the three kingdoms in heaven. The *Celestial* Kingdom was far and away the top prize, the highest rung. It was reserved for only the most righteous Mormons, and, of course, only Mormons. The *Terrestrial* Kingdom was the next step down. If your level of devotion was only fair to middling, or you were a Catholic or something, you'd probably wind up in the Terrestrial Kingdom, which wasn't too shabby, but not nearly as good as the Celestial, that's for sure. And if you were just downright wicked, you were most likely headed straight for the *Telestial* Kingdom. Not good.)

But why coffee? What was it about coffee that was so wicked? I never asked that question. Was it the caffeine? But Mormons devoured chocolate and that had caffeine, so maybe it was something else. I just didn't know. My mom would say it wasn't about the coffee. She'd say it was about the obedience. God could have just as easily outlawed, say, red licorice, or chicken noodle soup, because it wasn't about the "what", it was about the "why." And the why was to see if we would strictly obey our church leaders. It was a test of our blind obedience. Therefore, if church leaders said coffee was an abomination then, doggone it, coffee was abominable and Mormons must shun it. And so we did.

Notwithstanding the presumptive majesty of the Word of Wisdom, I worried that my Grandma West might be heading straight down the tubes of sin, and she was otherwise about as devout as they came. My mom had dropped me and a few of my brothers off at my grandma's house while she took another load of kids to the dentist. (The dentist was my uncle and he gave my parents a group discount. Whenever we'd have an appointment, we'd say that we'd been flossing regularly. This, of course, was a blatant lie and I'm sure he knew it when he couldn't wedge a string of floss between our teeth without a crowbar.) Anyway, we were in my grandma's backyard throwing apricots at her clothesline when I became bored and wandered into her kitchen.

There, right on her kitchen counter, in broad daylight, was a jar of Sanka. I was horrified. Mind you, it wasn't *real* coffee because it was decaffeinated. But it was close enough. I lifted the jar to be sure it was real, holding it away from my body like an undetonated hand grenade. I kept this ghastly secret to myself because I didn't want to rat out Grandma West to my mom who probably would have dropped dead had she seen it with her own two eyes. Besides, it was entirely possible that the jar of Sanka (which was half empty, by the way) belonged to a Catholic neighbor or something. At least I hoped so, for Grandma West's eternal sake.

All my friends were Mormon except one, a boy named Brad Grunwald. Actually, the Grunwalds *had* been Mormon but then quit going to church. We called people like that "In-actives" or "Jack Mormons". How Brother and Sister Grunwald could be inactive was a complete mystery to me. What had happened to these poor people? How could they *not* believe in the gold tablets? I mean, come on, a freaking *angel* had personally hand-delivered them for crying out loud! Helllloooo? Did they need to be hit over the head with the truth? I assumed the Grunwalds must've still believed, of course, but were just too lazy to keep the commandments.

But then, the shades of belief in Mormonism did span the spectrum, as I saw for myself. There were the hardcore believers who professed to know beyond a shadow of a doubt that every word the Prophet uttered, indeed every syllable, came straight from the lips of God, unfiltered. And there were the lackadaisical Mormons who didn't give it much thought—they just went through the motions. Still others picked and chose—the so-called smorgasbord Mormons. These people drove my mom nuts. "You don't get to pick and choose what to believe! That's not how it works. You either believe or you don't. There's no gray area."

Anyway, I was invited over to Brad's house for a summer barbeque. I was on guard because of their church inactivity and I didn't want it to rub off on me. They didn't even give a blessing on the food like my family did. (Dinners at our house were predictable. My mom would call us in from playing tag or tackle football in the front yard, smelling like autumn leaves with grass stains and dirty fingernails. There'd be non-matching place settings for each of us. We'd have tuna-noodle casserole with broken pieces of potato chips sprinkled on top. There'd usually be Del Monte cans of string beans or corn and perhaps something mixed with Cream of Mushroom soup. All 12 of us would sit around the massive table like it was the Last Supper with mis-matched water glasses, some glass, some plastic. My dad would randomly call on one of us to say the blessing on the food. Jane or Paul would belt it out in under five seconds. *Dear Heavenly Father, bless this food and thank you for it. Help it to nourish and strengthen our bodies and do us the good we need. In the name of Jesus Christ, Amen.* If it was said in any other order, or with any other words, we'd think that person was on the road to apostasy. The only exception would be when one of us, say, Julie, experimented with her righteousness by expanding on the food prayer, maybe doll it up by throwing in a few extra sentences to give it more oomph. *We love thee Heavenly Father and we know the church is true. Help us to keep thy commandments*, something like that. We'd peek out of the corner of our eyes wondering what had gotten into *her* as the casserole got cold. Great, you're more spiritual. We get it, okay? Now, please wrap it up so we can eat.)

At Brad's family barbeque, Brother Grunwald stood in their backyard over by the homemade fish pond with a can of beer in his hand. I knew he had to be drunker than a skunk. I watched him closely all evening long, waiting for the additional evidence of sin to expose itself. When would he swear? When would he start to slur his words and act weird? When would he proclaim a love for The Pill? When would he brag about seeing an R-rated movie? When would he slug one of his kids? When would he pin me down and try to pour beer down my throat?

Brother Grunwald hadn't done anything unusual by the time I left. I knew it was because he hid it so well. But still I was struck by the contradiction. Here was a nice man who scooped up the perfect amount of potato salad for me and put cheese on my hamburger just the way I liked it. Nevertheless, I knew you couldn't spit in God's eye and get away with it. Unless he repented, and did so quickly, Brother Grunwald could kiss the Celestial Kingdom goodbye. He was headed straight to the Terrestrial (I didn't see him dropping all the way down to the Telestial).

When I was a little older, I was able to differentiate between the evil of smoking a cigarette and the evil of first-degree murder. Exactly where a violation of the Word of Wisdom fit on the scale, I couldn't say. But I knew it was way up the list. Surely it ranked higher than, say, coveting. In any case, I knew that everything was weighed on the scales of sin.

———————

I overheard my dad talking to my mom about Sister Ellsworth down the street who had gallstones. I had no idea what a gallstone was (still don't) but it sounded pretty dire. My dad and Brother Olson next door had gone over to her house to give her a priesthood blessing.

I was taught early on about the healing power of priesthood blessings, administered to the sick by men who had been given special authority to act in God's name. The gift of the priesthood was special, I knew, but it wasn't at all rare—it was given to all 12-year-old boys in the church (girls didn't get it). The fact that every Mormon male with an ounce of testosterone had the priesthood didn't diminish its specialness for me.

Anyway, my dad was telling my mom that he and Brother Olson had gone over to give poor Sister Ellsworth the blessing just as her husband, Brother Ellsworth (about as inactive as they came), had stepped outside to have a cigarette. When he came back in, he joined in to give his wife this priesthood blessing (he was still technically a Mormon male). I'm not sure what the point of the story was, and why my dad was telling my mom about it, but I felt awful for Sister Ellsworth and her gallstones because everyone knew the healing powers wouldn't kick in if either the sick person, or the one giving the blessing, was unworthy. And I couldn't have imagined at the time anyone less worthy than Brother Ellsworth who'd basically sealed his wife's fate by having that cigarette. The way I saw it, the poor woman was toast.

Most Mormons I knew swore by the power of priesthood blessings. My experience, however, was spotty. In fact, I cannot honestly say I ever saw the blessings work. It was true that often times the person being blessed would eventually recover from the flu or stage a rally from the measles. But just as often the blessing seemed to fall flat, regardless of the amount of faith that went into it. The first blessing I ever gave is a case in point.

I was 19 years old with a stalwart belief, so stalwart that I went on a Mormon mission to Mexico for two years. By the way, there was never a doubt that I would go on a mission. One of the popular songs we sang in Sunday School was *I Hope They Call Me On A Mission!* It's a catchy little ditty that is faith inspiring, the sort of tune that compels you to want to go. All my friends had gone on missions or were going, indeed more than half the boys at Olympus High were going. It would have been far more difficult *not* to go. My parents, extended family, and friends would have thought I'd lost my marbles. What? Warren isn't going on a *mission?* Are you being serious? Did he knock someone up or something? That would be the only reason I wouldn't go—surely not because I'd lost my faith in the truth, because that would have been pure madness.

I'd been preaching in Mexico for a few months and my Spanish was, well, it was hit and miss. My companion suggested we go to Sister Ramirez's home because she was sick and needed a blessing. ("Companion" is what Mormons call the missionary who tags along because they proselytize in pairs, two by two, as most people probably know.) "Great, let's do it," I said. To be honest, I was itching to give a blessing because I'd never actually given one. I'd been given blessings from time to time, and I'd seen my dad and other men in the church give them, but I'd never officially administered one myself.

Sister Ramirez was in her late 80s and looked it. When we arrived, we found most of her extended family there—adult children, nieces, nephews, and a few other ward members. There were probably 20 people waiting for us missionaries to do our thing. I'll be honest here, there was some pressure.

Sister Ramirez was sitting in an old La-Z-Boy recliner with a multi-colored afghan on her lap. I put my hands on top of her gray head (that's how you do it) and began. Everyone in the room had their heads bowed in silent prayer, listening. I came through, big time. In fact, I gave one of the most awe-inspiring blessings I'd ever heard. It soared with aspirational rhetoric. I basically promised her that she would lick her present illness and live happily, for many more years to come.

When I finished, I took my hands off her head and stepped back to watch the magic. Would she leap from her chair and do some jumping jacks? Would she crack a clean joke, or sing a hymn? Maybe bake us some banana bread as a Thank You gesture? She was quiet and her adult daughter stepped forward and touched her on the shoulder. "Mom?" No response. "Mom? The missionaries are getting ready to leave now. Can you thank them for coming?" No response. "Mom?" She shook her again. Nothing.

She was dead. She had died *during* my fantastic blessing. I had basically killed her. Can you believe it? My companion looked at me with an expression that said one thing: We've gotta get outta here, fast. We excused ourselves while the family was still coming to grips with that fact that the missionaries had killed grandma. We hopped on our rusty bikes and pedaled like mad before rigor mortis set in back at the Ramirez home.

Word travelled in the mission like wildfire, and the word was simple and clear: Do not let Elder Driggs get near you with a blessing. He's liable to kill you. I couldn't decide if I had super powers, or no power at all.

How did I feel about this? I'd said all the right things. I even went the extra mile and spiced it up with eloquent things that I wished I'd recorded for future use because they were so stirring. And yet she died. Now, you might think that shook me. And it did, at least the part about her dying, for I was not a monster. But it didn't move the needle on my faith. I chalked it up to random bad luck, or the possibility that Sister Ramirez had sealed her own fate by sneaking off for a cup of coffee. The best I could fathom was that it had more to do with what God wanted than what I wanted. I figured I could jazz up the language until I was blue in the face, really give it a jolt of literary flourish, and it wouldn't matter if God had other ideas.

9

MY FRIEND, GLEN LINDQUIST, INVITED ME TO a BYU football game when I was 10. The Cougars were playing San Jose State and beat them when a BYU player returned a kickoff 100 yards for the win. It was pretty exciting. But it wasn't the football game that caught my attention that day. It was the black armbands that every single player on San Jose State's team wore. What was the meaning of this, I wondered?

I asked Brother Lindquist who lived a few doors down from us on Siggard Drive. "Oh, it's nothing," he said between bites of a hot dog. "Just a bunch of people who can't mind their own danged business."

Their own business? About what? I asked my dad about it later that night. He said the players on the other team were protesting the Mormon church's refusal to give black men the priesthood. I don't remember exactly how I reacted to that, but I don't suppose I cared a whole lot at the time. As far as I knew, there was a perfectly good reason why black people were being discriminated against, which all had to do with the War in Heaven.

If you've never heard of the War in Heaven, it was the war of all wars—a titanic Battle Royale for our very lives, quite literally. You could pretty much forget about the Big Bang theory, or any other man-made theory about how it all came to be, because Mormons know it all started with the War in Heaven, the Super Bowl of Creation with God as the sole referee.

I was taught that before we were born here on earth, we lived as spirits up in heaven as God's children (God was our dad but there was scant information about our mom, which I thought was unfair, especially if she was like most moms who did all the work and then got blamed for everyone's therapy). All of us, every single one of us, lived together as one gigantic family—Hitler, Jesus, Genghis Khan, you, me, Cher—you name it. God had a glorified body of flesh and bones, but we didn't—we were just spirits, like angels, so you could basically put your hand right through us. We wanted to be like God with a real body.

As God was formulating his plan to send us to earth to get our bodies, he became hung up on whether to give each of us our own free agency—the right to misbehave, as it were—once we landed on earth. He looked to Jesus and Lucifer, his two favorite children, to help settle the issue. God loved his children equally, but he put this important question to those two because they were the most prominent spirit children of all.

Lucifer argued that because God loved all of his spirit children, he ought to ensure that we would all come down to earth, behave, die, and return to heaven, unblemished by sin. This seemed like a sensible plan. Jesus, on the other hand, argued that we ought to be given free agency. If we lived righteously and obeyed the commandments, then super, we would return to live with our heavenly parents. If we didn't, we wouldn't make it back to the

Celestial Kingdom (we'd be slated for a lesser kingdom like the Terrestrial, or, God forbid, the Telestial). This also seemed like a sensible plan.

God put the two plans to a democratic vote. A vote for Jesus meant you'd come down to earth with your newly minted body and have free agency to do whatever you wanted (and hopefully you'd be smart enough to listen to God's commandments so you could return to heaven), and a vote for Lucifer meant you'd come down to earth, be wired to automatically behave, and then return to God's loving arms. That's when it got nasty, so nasty in fact that a war broke out over these two competing proposals.

Jesus's side won the war. There was no record of the final vote tally, so we don't know if it was a nail biter or a landslide victory. But we do know that Lucifer hated the result of the vote and wanted nothing to do with the program. In fact, he was such a poor sport that he stormed off and took those who'd voted for his plan with him. God then proclaimed that anyone who'd voted for Jesus, the victor, would be allowed to come down to earth and get their body. Those who voted for Lucifer would not, including Lucifer himself. Those who'd voted for Lucifer were cast off to become spirit demons—Demons of Darkness who would torment their earthly siblings, trying to scare them and get them to sin, for they were sore losers. They would be like the spirits who took over that girl's body in *The Exorcist*.

This, to me as a child, seemed like a pretty harsh result for choosing the wrong candidate. I wondered if there was more to it than that, if God somehow knew ahead of time that our spirit siblings who'd voted for Lucifer's plan were bad seeds, awful children from the get-go. But that was mere childhood speculation on my part.

But here's how this related to the black arm bands. You see, there were also spirits in heaven who couldn't quite make up their minds about who to vote for, the ones who dilly-dallied before finally, and perhaps reluctantly, casting their vote for Jesus. God gave them the benefit of the doubt and let them come to earth and get a body, but there was a catch, a price to be paid. These dilly-dalliers were cursed with a dark skin. That's the price they paid for being so wishy-washy about Jesus.

The net result of the War in Heaven, then, was that people who voted for Jesus right off the bat were given white skin. White people were the ones who got behind Jesus from the get-go. People of color did not. Sure, they eventually came around and voted for him (we knew that because they were here on earth with bodies and weren't a bunch of evil spirits), but they dragged their feet. They sat on the fence for too long, wringing their hands over who to vote for. The skin curse was the consequence for that ambivalence, and it would serve as a reminder to anyone who cared that they'd been slackers when it came to their initial commitment to Jesus.

The skin curse was a nasty one, so God didn't just throw it around willy-nilly. Only when it was dire. I didn't have a clue why the Lamanites skin was a different shade than, say, Latinos or Asians (remember, Lamanites were the Native American Indians who could trace their swarthy skin back to Laman, the disobedient son from The Book of Mormon who got on God's wrong side). My Mormon education was unclear on those nuances. Perhaps those slightly less-dark people sat on the fence a split-second shorter before casting their ballot for Jesus. I just didn't know.

So, there you have it. The War in Heaven was why Mormons could not in good faith give black men the priesthood. They had misbehaved in the spirit world before they were born, not flagrantly mind you, but just bad enough. And the football team from San Jose State wore black arm bands when they played BYU, in protest of this doctrine.

Growing up, I was vaguely aware that my church promised Native Americans their skin would turn lighter if they accepted Mormonism. I don't remember if the church taught that was also an option for African Americans. It became moot in 1978 when the Prophet had a revelation that God had decided to lift the ban and allow black men to hold the priesthood. Most Mormons rejoiced at the time, and sincerely so. But there were some hold-outs—old-time racists who believed black peoples' pre-mortal sins should not be so easily pardoned. And there were others who believed God wouldn't have arbitrarily changed his mind like that.

I didn't look at revelation as God "changing his mind." I believed he spoke to the Mormon prophet in real time, telling him how to steer the ship. This elasticity was faith-promoting to me—it just made sense. After all, who'd want to belong to a church that was trapped in a Stone Age box, forced forevermore to defend the ideas that might've fit an earlier age, but didn't fit now? It was comforting to know that we were always up-to-date on exactly what God wanted, and when he wanted it.

———————

Coy was the only black kid I'd ever met. We were both in the seventh grade. I felt sorry for Coy. What, I wondered, had he done in the pre-earth spirit world to have merited being slapped with the skin curse? Something awful, I presumed at the time. I asked my Sunday School teacher about it. "Don't worry," she said. "God loves all his children, even negros. I'm sure his skin will gradually turn whiter as he repents." This made me feel a little better at the time because Coy was a good kid. I wanted to reassure him that one day, if he kept being good, he could be like me.

Did my Sunday School teacher really believe that? If so, did she feel superiority, or did she feel shame? I didn't ask myself those questions at the time. In fact, all the adults I knew presumably believed the same thing. And why not? It was in the Mormon doctrine that came straight from the lips of Abraham, probably the biggest headliner in the Bible next to Jesus. After all, it was Abraham's hand-written mummy scroll that was the primary source of Mormon doctrine on this topic. I assumed Abraham knew what he was talking about because he was such a Biblical superstar (even though it had sorta shocked me that he'd come so close to stabbing his own son, Isaac, to death on the altar before God stopped him at the last second).

Many years later, we had an elderly man over to our home for dinner. There was a basketball game on television and this man was watching it with me and my teenage sons. My son asked him who he was rooting for. "The Celtics," the elderly man said. "Why them?" my son asked. The man looked at my son and simply said: "Because they have more white players." My teenage sons, who'd been largely unaware of the melanin count, looked at this old man like he was from Mars. He wasn't, though—he was from the Valley View 5th ward.

———————

My identity, growing up, had mostly to do with being a Mormon. However, I also understood that we were Republicans. I wasn't sure what it meant, but I instinctively knew it must've been good to be a Republican.

Utah wasn't much of a red state in those days. In fact, when I was growing up, Utah leaned blue. We elected Democratic Governors for 20 straight years. Same thing with our Senator and a majority of our state legislature. Utah's electoral votes went to FDR, Truman, and LBJ, all Democrats. But then the abortion question came along and it flipped the state from blue to red almost overnight. Mormons would not, simply could not, support a woman's right to choose, and Utah has been red ever since. These days, Republicans win by merely brandishing their Pro-Life credentials, whether they're running for Congress or dog catcher. Take my mom. It would not matter if the Republican candidate was an idiot, as long as he was Pro-Life. (Mormons support the right to choose, provided it is the right choice.)

When I was a boy, however, Mormons voted for Democrats without any shame whatsoever. Of course, plenty of them voted for Republicans too, like my parents. I recall being over at Steve's house across the street one day. His mom (the exotic sunbather) was on the phone, the cord stretched all the way from the wall in their kitchen to the dining room so she could watch Steve's older brother mowing the lawn. His other brothers were running through the house playing cowboys and Indians and the phone cord was so taut it could have easily beheaded an Apache. I overheard her talking about the upcoming presidential election and how Goldwater was going to win in a landslide over LBJ. (I must have been 8 because that election was in 1964.) Her prediction was comforting because I'd overheard my parents talking about how LBJ was bad news indeed. It turned out to be a landslide all right, one of the biggest ever, but, regrettably, it went the other way.

Sure enough, my parents had been spot-on about LBJ and his antics because he went and passed the Civil Rights Amendment, something only a flaming liberal would do. And within a few years after that we had to weather the dreaded Equal Rights Amendment, which my 17-year old sister, Julie, marched against. I was two years younger than she was at the time, and didn't know much about it. I asked her why she was waking up so early on a Saturday to do such a thing. "I just heard it's bad," she said. I wanted to know how she'd heard about it. "Oh, the bishop told all of us girls in the ward that it was bad because pretty soon men could come into women's bathrooms and women would have to go to war and stuff like that. That's why he wants us to go march against it down at the state capitol. So, we're all car-pooling down there."

This is the way it was. Obedience. There was no need for independent thought. Why bother to learn about the basis for a commandment? If the bishop said to do it, you did. The heavy thinking had already been done for you. If you questioned it, you were on the slippery slope to apostasy, and nobody wanted to slide down *that* ride. This protest march was a feather in my sister's spiritual cap. She was blindly doing something she'd been asked to do without complaint, marching against equal rights for her own gender.

I was 15 and had no axe to grind since I was a boy. Besides, I wanted to sleep in. But still I wondered why they would march against the Equal Rights Amendment. It sounded pretty benign to me, laudable even. I mean, the *Equal Rights* Amendment? Who wouldn't root for that? And why would a woman be opposed to it, I wondered? My mom said it was the principle of the thing. The principle of the thing? To march against equal rights? It was?

No, she said, the principle of the thing was to do what the church leaders asked. Period. Ours was not to question. It wouldn't have mattered if we'd been asked to march against civil rights, the prohibition of same-sex marriage, or apple pie. The subject matter of what was being asked, or the rational basis behind it, was beside the point.

I was over at my friend Eric's house for dinner one night when the subject of the Equal Rights Amendment came up (as it often did in those days). I remember Eric's mom, Sister Harmon, asking her husband, who was sitting at the head of the table with his arms folded, "So, honey, what exactly do we believe about the ERA?"

10

I WAS NEVER A SUPERB ATHLETE. SURE, I could throw a spiral and I was a whiz at second base, but I was never a jock. This was plainly evident by the time I was 6.

My aunt Beverly lived on a farm in Pleasant Grove, a sleepy agricultural hamlet that is 20 miles south of Salt Lake City. Every year they held a rodeo at their farm. I thought it was a big event but when I think back on it now, there were probably only a handful of neighborhood kids in cowboy shirts along with a few moms. I was entered in the bull riding contest. This was a misnomer. The bull was actually a small brown calf that undoubtedly struggled to hold the weight of my scrawny 50-pound frame. You know a cow is docile when it has been given a name, like a family pet. The calf I was about to ride was named Mama's Girl; nonetheless I was scared to death. I hurtled to the ground which was all of three feet away. I could not even hang on for eight seconds to a calf named Mama's Girl, but I was given a ribbon anyway. It must've been one of those participation ribbons, the kind you get no matter what. I was embarrassed to display it because I knew, deep down, that I was a fraud.

My next athletic achievement was baseball, and I was actually pretty good. I made the little league All-Stars every year. I was on the Titans and Steve's dad was the coach. We played our games at Evergreen Park, a sloping lawn with potholes and a backstop with holes that someone had fixed by jerry-rigging some wire into the biggest gaps.

I took Little League seriously. There were four teams in our league: Titans, Giants, Flyers, and Lions. If the game started at five in the evening, I'd put my uniform on at noon, to be good and ready. We weren't allowed to go swimming on "game days" so as not to tire ourselves out. I assumed our coach was every bit as invested as we were—how he must have been strategizing all day at work over the batting order and who would be the starting pitcher. When he'd show up just two minutes before the game, I figured he must've been plotting all that time.

The coach of the Giants was intense (as in plumb crazy). One game, I was playing third base and his team was up to bat. His player hit a long fly ball down the sloping hill and the batter tried to stretch it out for a triple. He slid into third base and I tagged him. It was a close play, I admit, and could have gone either way, but the 16-year-old umpire called him out and the Giant's coach went ape shit. The teenage ump changed his call to safe to mollify the coach and then it was our coach's turn to get mad. The poor kid didn't know what to do, looking back and forth between these two red-faced grown men with curled fists and prominent veins in their foreheads. He finally decided his initial call had been correct and pronounced the Giant out, once and for all.

Oh my, the Giant's coach was apoplectic, spittle flying. "I'll see to it that you never call another game! You hear me!" He then laid down on the ground on the third base line next to me and started pounding the grass with his fists. I am not kidding. This was as much drama as I'd ever seen in my whole life. I was mesmerized by this man, who had to be at least 40 years old, kicking and screaming like a toddler having a meltdown in the toy aisle at Walmart.

Soon other parents were involved, trying to restrain him. Our coach called us off the field where we huddled at a safe distance. He told us not to look, so we all looked. I knew the umpire's call at third base was close, and I knew it was a big out for us because the Giants were in first place and we were their biggest rivals, but I didn't think it warranted this sort of tantrum. Sure, maybe the stink eye directed at the teenage ump, or a modest swear word muttered under his breath that only those really close to him could have heard. But, no, not this. I've since wondered what happened to this man. I presume he's had a heart attack by now. I knew him only as Brother Waldrum, Coach of the Giants, who lived in the Valley View Sixth ward.

But when I think back on my games up there at Evergreen Park, I don't really think about that guy. Instead, I can see my mom. She is sitting on a blue patchwork quilt on the grass, a baby, maybe Ben or Matt, in her lap. She is alone. All the other moms and dads are sitting a fair distance away. It's just my mom. I have no idea where all the other kids are. I never gave her much credit for supporting me as a boy. I don't remember her helping me with homework or buying the soft bar of soap I really needed to carve that sculpture in my seventh-grade art class. But there she was, at every game, without fail.

I still have the letter she wrote me after we lost the championship game. A flyball had ricocheted off Brent Downard's glove in the bottom of the sixth inning and bounced over the leftfield fence for the game-winning homer. I was crushed.

August 2, 1968

To my darling son, Warren. Today was the day you lost the All Star baseball game. The score was 1-0 in the bottom of the sixth and the East Millcreek team got a runner on base. Then the big moment came—the batter hit a ball over the left field fence and they won the game 2-1. I have never in my life cried over a baseball game until tonight. I know how much that game meant to you. It was the climax to four wonderful years of Little League baseball that I was lucky enough to watch you go through. How proud you were of that uniform! And how proud I am of you!

I am so sorry that you are hurting now. I wish I could take the pain from you. But it will be all right. I promise. Big things are in store for you and I can't wait to watch you from the sidelines for as long as I live. What a remarkable son you are. Don't tell the other kids, but you're my favorite.

I love you so much,
Mom

I think back now at how harried she must have been. Ten children. Not much money. Chaos. I think of her sitting down to write that letter. Where was she? In her bedroom? In the laundry room surrounded by 10 loads of wash? In the kitchen after all of us were finally asleep? My dad is always the hero in my stories—my mom the unsung. But he wasn't at my games.

———

My mom liked baseball but she wasn't crazy about me playing little league football. I broached the subject one late-summer afternoon. She was down in the basement, stacks of folded laundry everywhere, standing on the newfangled exercise equipment that was a weight-loss no-brainer. I was surprised my parents bought it because they weren't big on fitness or spending money on appliances, and especially for something as vain as losing weight. Maybe you remember these contraptions. It looked like a treadmill but instead of a revolving track there was a six-inch band that you strapped around your waist while standing face-forward like you would on a treadmill. Then you were supposed to lean back slightly so your waist was supported by the band. That's when the magic happened. You simply turned on the machine and the band jiggled you. That's it. The band jiggled the crap out of your midsection where all the fat was.

Anyway, I was downstairs and my mom was on the machine, trying to jiggle the fat away. "Mom, can I join little league football?" I asked. "IIII dddooonnn'ttt thhhiiinnnkkk tthhaaatts aaa goooood iiiddeeaaa," she said. Later, I got her to agree, but she said I would have to pay the sign-up fee. I was prepared for this because I had usually paid for my Little League baseball sign-ups from all my jobs.

I could lie and tell you I was a ferocious tackler, a one-man wrecking crew, but I wasn't. I'm a pacifist and I should have known that I'd never be Dick Butkus, but Howard and Eric were trying out so I figured I might as well give it a whirl. On the day of tryouts, they lined everyone up and put them through a bunch of testosterone-laden drills. The coaches then drew straws for drafting order and then went around the horn picking their teams. I don't think their goal was to publicly humiliate me but I was one of the last boys picked, out of charity, and only because I had paid my $25.00. Even the doughy fat kids who could barely run were picked ahead of me because at least they could squat on the offensive line, impenetrable mounds of immovable blubber.

I pedaled my bike to practice every afternoon. Never missed. The coaches (there were about five of them—dads who longed to be tough again and wanted to impose their brand of toughness on us eighth graders like this was the Battle of the Bulge). The practices sucked. We had to run and hit and do push-ups until it was dark. If someone missed a tackle the whole team had to run a lap. Everyone hated me for that. But I was no quitter.

I don't know how many games we had that season, maybe 10. They were Saturday mornings and half the time it was cold and rainy. I'd stand on the sidelines, at once hoping the coach would put me in, and hoping he wouldn't. He didn't. He never did.

Our reward for enduring the season was a trip to Long Beach, California to play a team down there a few days after Thanksgiving. We earned the money for the trip by selling frozen turkeys, door to door. I was sick and tired of hauling those 20-pound frozen turkeys around (and seems I sold the most, I had the most to haul around).

There are three things I'd like to say about this Long Beach experience, not necessarily in order of relevance.

First: It was the first time I had ever been on an airplane. I thought it was amazing, except for the fact that I was sitting directly in front of a chain smoker. He was in the smoking section and I was one row ahead of him in the non-smoking section. The guy didn't appear to give a hoot about the Word of Wisdom and I figured his sinning would give me a wicked case of lung cancer.

Second: Colin West and I stayed with the family of a boy

on the other team, a cocky kid who sassed his parents. They were Catholic (I'd never even met a Catholic before, but knew I had to be wary of them) and their house was like a Gallery of Christianity. Take the living room, for example, which was a virtual shrine to Jesus. There were paintings of Jesus, charcoals of Jesus, and woodcarvings of Jesus. You would have thought Jesus lived there. And the sheer number of crosses! Some were handsomely carved, complete with a desperately pained Jesus wearing nothing but a twisted loincloth around his waist, and there were empty ones without him. Some dramatically dripped fake blood. This didn't necessarily creep me out, but we Mormons weren't big cross people. We believed in Jesus, because we were Christians too, but we were more likely to portray him in happier times, like when he was walking on water or doling out the fish.

Anyway, this Catholic family hauled us to Mass (they couldn't leave us unsupervised at their house because we might have stolen something, started a fire, or sued them for abandonment). Colin and I reluctantly went along. There came a point in the Mass when we were supposed to kneel during a prayer (which, to be honest, sounded like a séance to me). I was horrified. Should I do it, I wondered? Should I kneel in a church that was the devil's playground? Would that be disloyal? This felt like spiritual roulette. I had always been taught that the Catholic church was The Great and Abominable Church, and yet there I was, on the verge of kneeling in it. I looked sideways at Colin. Would he do it? Would he prostrate himself before the devil? He did and I followed suit. I felt like Peter must've felt after he flat out denied knowing Jesus three times.

Third: The Game. I can't remember if we won or lost, and I didn't care. It was rainy and muddy. I had hardly played the entire season, despite my devotion. As the clock ticked down, my coach, an awful man (may he rot in the Telestial Kingdom), looked down the sideline and saw me. There were two minutes left in the game. "Driggs, go in at left safety!"

I ran in with my jersey and pants that were as white at the driven snow when all the others were soaked the color of mud. Nothing happened on the first play. It was a run and the guy didn't come anywhere near me, thank God. The next play was a pass, but a bad one, sort of in my direction. The receiver ran into me quite by accident (probably because I wasn't in the correct position). I fell down to the mud when he bumped into me. The game ended.

We all went into the locker room where the coach gathered us around for his season-ending pep talk. He called out the heroics of our quarterback and everyone else on the team. It was rah-rah-piss-boom-bah, slaps on the back, and all the rest. He had nearly wound down with this aspirational speech when he spotted me in the corner. "Hey, look everybody!" and he pointed at me. "Even Driggs got a little dirt on his uniform!" And he laughed. Everyone turned to see my shame.

A few years later, after I received my driver's license, I bought a dozen Grade A eggs from my newspaper-route money and drove by his house late at night. I knew I shouldn't do it. I knew it was an immature response to an injustice, but it really felt good. My aim was perfect, so perfect in fact that I should have been the star quarterback.

11

WE OWNED A PIANO, A MAPLE-COLORED UPRIGHT that sat against the wall of our living room beneath one of my mom's oil paintings. The painting was of a vase of roses and it was actually quite good. (Her painting phase was followed by an extended toile painting phase. I don't know if this was a nationwide fad, or just something my mom cooked up on her own. I also don't know where she found the time to take so many small wooden boxes, boards, and knick-knacks and glue a picture or decal on them. Then she'd put about 20 coats of shellac on these masterpieces. I still have a few of them and they are not for sale.)

She helped me make a container to take to my third-grade class on Valentine's Day. It was a Folger's can (perish the thought!) that we painted pink and then turned on its side to make it look like a pig. We cut a slot in the top of the pig's back for the Valentine cards, like a mailbox, and then I shellacked the bejesus out of it. She wrote "Be My ValenSwine" on the side. I didn't get it because I didn't know what a swine was, but she said it made sense.

Anyway, I decided I wanted to play our piano so my mom negotiated with Mrs. Martel down the street for lessons. Please note that this was *Mrs.* Martel and not *Sister* Martel. That's because she wasn't a Mormon; one of the few Gentiles in the neighborhood. Mrs. Martel had big red hair and a widow's peak as severe as Eddie Munster's. I always thought it made her face look like a heart. She was nice and her house always smelled like coffee. Notwithstanding her patient tutelage, I could never get past *The Wigwam* (a precursor to chop sticks). I'd bang the keys on that damned piano for hours at a time, always playing *The Wigwam* which basically consisted of banging the same keys over and over, to replicate the sound of an authentic Indian war dance. The only reason this did not infuriate the rest of my family (but maybe it did, I just don't remember) was because the general din in our house was already north of piercing.

We were 10 kids who made the noise of 20. We all ran around yelling our heads off like bandits with bandanas tied around our mouths and noses. We jumped on the spring-less sofa that had once been beige and played tag throughout the house. There were gouges in the walls and nicks in all the door jams. There was a constant barrage of Indian burns, wet willies, and musical arm-pit farts. At least one of us always had the croup, or pink eye.

I suppose we were simply trying to get some attention from our beleaguered parents. We made maudlin displays of our bruises and scabs to be recognized. We hollered overly dramatic things, like "Steve stole my baseball cards!" or "Andy farted in my face!" or "Paul almost swore!" or "Danny came at me with a butcher knife!" These were true statements. My parents weren't about to get involved in a minor skirmish like someone farting in our face, but the butcher knife might have raised an eyebrow, had they known about it.

My mom was always trying to get us to go outside and play. And we did. In fact, we spent most of our time outside inventing things to do because there wasn't much to do in the house (remember, we didn't have a TV). We only went back inside to pee (if the house was fairly close, otherwise we'd look furtively around as we stood behind a lilac). My mom was onto us, too. No matter where she was in the house, she had a knack for hearing us come in and she'd yell: "Hit the target for once!"

We made more forts than the U.S. Army during the Civil War. We dug holes, chucked dirt clods at each other, caught bugs, shot hoops, spied on people, and doorbell ditched. Frankly, we terrorized the neighborhood.

When the ice cream truck with its melodic jingle would drive down our street, we'd pause and stare at it with longing, for we could never afford such a luxury (or, come to think of it, maybe we could and my mom was just afraid the driver might be a pervert). I was always hungry. We had things to eat, but who wanted to live on a wilted carrot or handful of puffed wheat? (Potato chips? Twinkies? Sugar cereal? What, are you kidding me?) I do recall a package of Fig Newtons that lasted about two minutes.

I grew up in an era before the proliferation of fast food (McDonald's opened its first restaurant the year I was born). We went out to eat as a family, but it was exceedingly rare. Rare as in hardly ever. My parents said we couldn't afford it, and I had no reason to disbelieve them. But it also might have had something to do with coordinating the effort to haul that many children anywhere, much less to an establishment that would've shuddered to see all of us marching in to buy the cheapest thing on the laminated menu, and then share it, leaving the scooted-together tables looking like Dresden after the Germans finished with it.

There was a local hamburger joint named Arctic Circle that was located about a mile from our house. One day my mom, who must have been high on something, said we could go there (it wasn't even someone's birthday, or a baptism). I volunteered to ride my bike to pick up the hamburgers. And that is all I was supposed to buy: 10 hamburgers. No French fries or shakes or anything. Just 10 hamburgers.

I pedaled my bike up the hill, past the junior high school and to Artic Circle, my mouth watering. My bike was a Red Flyer and weighed about half a ton. I'd gotten it for my birthday and it was the nicest present I ever received. I'm not entirely sure it was new when my parents bought it, but it was new to me.

I ordered the burgers and they were delivered to me in a white paper sack. It was a large sack but 10 burgers filled it up, so the top of the bag could be rolled over only once. The following year I would install a wire basket to the front of my handlebars for my newspaper route, but at the time it was basket-less, which meant I had to hold the paper sack and steer at the same time.

I pedaled home, balancing the sack on my lap without incident until I got to the hill on Siggard Drive. I was hugging the right side of the road, up next to the gutter. For some reason, I put my head down, perhaps to pedal harder because I knew I would be hailed a hero as soon as I walked in our door with that sack of burgers. I looked up when I got to Mark Layton's house, but not in time, for there was a car parked parallel to the curb. I ran into the back of it at full steam, flew over the handlebars, and landed on the road surrounded by buns, ketchup, hamburger patties, pickles, and a few napkins.

There was no other traffic on the road and no witnesses. I was scraped up pretty bad, but I had no broken bones. Obviously, I wasn't wearing a helmet because nobody had heard of them way back then. I panicked when I came to my senses and saw the strewn burgers. My brothers would kill me. I couldn't let them down. I hobbled up and picked the hamburgers off the pavement, re-wrapped them, and got back on my bike. The paper sack had ripped so I had a few of them in my pocket and balanced the remainder in the partial sack as best I could. My front tire was bent from the wreck, but I made it home a few minutes later, my front tire wobbling and my forearms covered with blood and road rash.

My siblings pounced on those burgers like there was a famine. They didn't notice the small pieces of gravel or the tarry taste. When all the burgers were gone someone noticed my scraped arms and the blood on my shirt. "What happened to you?" they asked. "Nothing," I said as I pulled a partial hamburger from my pocket and ate it right in front of them. I guess they weren't curious why I'd had it in my pocket.

———

It was during this time that I was cruel to someone. Being cruel to anyone, and especially someone who wasn't cool or popular, was about the worst thing you could do in my family. It was right up there with smoking.

There was a boy named Jason King who lived a few doors down. The regal name didn't fit him. He was chubby and wore thick glasses, things that we thought justified being ditched. To top it off, he wore headgear out in public, something only a loser would do. We'd call him to play and then hide in the bushes when he showed up, meandering around looking for us. "Hey, Warren, where are you guys?" We'd be whispering in the bushes, "Asonjay is a omohay." (This was during our homophobic and Pig Latin phases).

My mom was devasted when Jason's mom called her to report on the abuse. I felt pretty stupid in front of my parents because

I knew that if they stood for anything, it was kindness. And especially to someone who needed it more than others. I was told that I would immediately pedal my bike over to Jason's house. But what will I do when I get there, I asked? What do you think you'll do? I dunno, apologize, I guess. You certainly will. He'll be at your next sleepover, too, and you'll sit with him at lunch.

The hallmark of charity in our house was to be kind to the outcast. That is why, when I was asked to the high school Christmas dance by Susan Gilmore in our ward, a homely girl with big-time acne, my mom insisted that I say yes, immediately, and be happy about it, even though word on the street was that the most popular girl at school was going to ask me the next day. My dad would've been clueless about the whole affair, but had he known he would have turned it into a morality play: "Warren, you are the most amazing boy of all. Always remember that people look up to you, so if you embrace her, then everyone else will too." My mom wouldn't have beat around the bush. She wouldn't have bothered with that sort of nobility speech— she just told me what I was going to do. "And don't you think for one second that you're better than her, Buster. Not for one second. Now you'll go and you'll make sure she has a nice time. Are we clear?"

Susan came to the door to pick me up for the dance and allow me to give her a corsage. I had previously been instructed that I was to invite her in, like a gentleman. I agreed, on the condition that my mom not say anything stupid. Meanwhile, my mom had cut two holes in the newspaper and was sitting on the sofa, holding the newspaper up in front of her, spying on us through the holes. My mom.

———

I took a summer-school typing class in conjunction with piano. Even though we didn't have a typewriter (and computers were light years away) my mom thought typing would be a good skill to learn. I was a good typist. I could rattle off "Now is the time for all good men to come to the aid of their country" in less than five seconds. I'd type it over and over again, my fingers flying across the keyboard. I barely even had to look.

The boy I sat next to in summer school (which, by the way, was the height of cruelty—to make a kid go to summer school) was named Rick Clissold. He was a tall, lanky boy with bangs, handsome in a George-Harrison-with-better-teeth sort of way. One day he didn't show up for class. I figured he was probably out swimming which is what you were *supposed* to do during summer vacation. He missed the remainder of the summer-school term, and then didn't show up for the start of sixth grade. I didn't think much of it until I finally saw him after the Christmas vacation. His right leg had been amputated, above the knee. He walked with crutches and his pant leg was pinned up, like a soldier returning from war. It was the most awful thing I'd ever seen.

Rick finished the school year and the novelty of the boy on crutches faded until he became just another kid after a while. And then he died. Cancer. I didn't know what cancer was until that time.

The worst thing to come to grips with was the fact that the Clissolds weren't Mormons, so I figured Rick wouldn't be able to go to heaven. And he'd been a good kid. I remember feeling angry toward his parents (who I didn't even know) because they had allowed their family to drift so far from the truth. Now look what you've done, Mr. and Mrs. Clissold! I hope you're happy. Gol, your son can't even go to heaven because you didn't join the church when you had the chance. But then, on the other hand, I had an overwhelming sense of compassion for them, for I could not imagine losing a child. Worse yet, I figured they didn't believe in life after death because they weren't Mormon, so they probably assumed they would never see their son again.

Where did it come from, my certainty that we Mormons had an exclusive corner on the truth? Was I complicit in my own beliefs? It would not be entirely fair to say it all had been foisted upon me, that I'd been compelled to believe or be killed. Then again, that *is* what I'd been taught, spiritually speaking; that my everlasting salvation was at stake. I do know that none of my beliefs originated with me, because I didn't have much original thought until I was about 25 years old. I accepted what I was told and did so without an ounce of critical reflection. Not an ounce.

How, I wondered, could people *not* believe? My goodness, Donnie and Marie Osmond were members of the church! What more proof did you need? And don't forget about Ezra Taft Benson who served as Secretary of the Interior during the Eisenhower administration. We had him too. My parents, my friends, my teachers, my doctors, my grandparents. They all believed. How on earth could nearly every adult I knew be wrong?

But I did more than merely accept these beliefs. I embraced them. I bore strong testimony to their authenticity. When I was a teenager and first started dating Cindy, her brother-in-law was a disbeliever. I figured he was either too lazy to keep the commandments or his sinning had spiraled wildly out of control to the point that the spirit had abandoned him, leaving him no choice but to wander aimlessly in a spiritual wasteland. He only *thought* he was happy, but he didn't fool me.

I could not imagine accepting the faith of another church. A belief in other churches or dogma, even Christian churches, felt like an obscenity to me. There was a wary suspicion in Mormonism toward other churches. They weren't dens of iniquity, per se, but we had to be careful because we knew Satan zeroed in on God's chosen people. Naturally, he'd want nothing more than to beguile one of us Mormons to his side. If you had no belief you might wind up in hell, but if you were disloyal enough to worship in another church you might go there just as quickly. There was a loyalty to Mormonism, and only to Mormonism.

I was told the church was the fastest growing wave on earth—a mighty surge that would eventually drench the world. This was inspiring and made me proud to be a Mormon. When I was a boy, there were about two million Mormons in the United States, which seemed like a lot to me. Coincidentally, there were about the same number of Jews. The Mormons and Jews also have nearly identical numbers worldwide these days—about 15 million each. So, as it turns out, God's New Chosen People are pacing along nicely with his Old Chosen People.

I wasn't a bit surprised to be told how fast Mormonism was growing, and my loyalty to Mormonism was unflinching. I was so sure, so *adamant*, of my rightness. I had been shown the truth by the Holy Spirit which I knew was much stronger than any man-made explanation or so-called scientific enlightenment. But had I ever truly felt the spirit? I suppose I had. I suppose there were times while singing a hymn when I was touched. But I had the same feeling when I watched a Hallmark movie, or sang America the Beautiful. Did that mean they were also true?

12

ERIC SNOW'S 4-YEAR-OLD SISTER FELL OUT of the back seat of their moving car at the bottom of Siggard Drive. I was in the car and witnessed the whole thing. His mom must've turned the wheel too hard and the door flew open and out she went. These things happen, but what was crazy is she fell into an open garbage can. Eric's mom slammed on the brakes, we all jumped out to get his little sister, and there she was, in a galvanized steel garbage can that someone had left the lid off of.

This little girl didn't need to go to the doctor and I wondered if Sister Snow even bothered to tell Brother Snow about it. Even as a young boy I realized there are some things better left unsaid between husband and wife. I wouldn't have dreamed of criticizing Sister Snow's marriage or her parenting skills (or even her driving skills for that matter), but you had to wonder. Maybe it was the guilt that prompted her to take Eric and his little sister to the Evergreen swimming pool later that afternoon. She said I could come too. Perhaps this was to buy my silence, I cannot say.

When I later reported this episode to my family, they scoffed. There's no way that could happen, they said. Fall out of a moving car and into a garbage can? Impossible. These were the same people who believed without any doubt whatsoever that an angel delivered a stack of gold tablets and magic spectacles to Joseph Smith. Would they have been more likely to believe me if I'd wrapped it up inside a religious story? What if I'd said the car was on fire and this little girl earnestly prayed to escape the inferno and her prayers were answered when the heavens opened and an angel in a white flowing robe came down, flung open the car door, and gently plopped her into a safe steel garbage can? Then would they have believed me?

Anyway, we were at the pool later that afternoon. After about an hour, I saw the lifeguard dive into the pool and swim as fast as he could to the area right beneath the rope that separates the shallow and deep ends. He came up with Eric's little sister. Now, I am colorblind, so my confidence in shades is low, but she looked blue to me. Her eyes were closed and the lifeguard hurried over to the side of the pool where he laid her down on the hot cement. He started doing mouth-to-mouth resuscitation on her as people began to crowd around. Somebody was yelling to call an ambulance which came and the men in uniform took over. She survived. In fact, they didn't even take her away in the ambulance.

I reflected later on Eric's little sister and her crazy day. What did it mean, if anything? Falling out of a moving car and into an open garbage can, and then almost drowning a few hours later? Was it a sign that her days were numbered, or was it simply a 24-hour black cloud? She was so young I didn't honestly think it was related to any sinning she'd done, but it seemed like there should have been *some* explanation.

Mormonism tried to answer all the big questions, even the ones that were unanswerable. Not knowing was uncomfortable and disorienting. That's why we were determined to have a ready answer for everything, even if we had to make it up on the fly. Fortunately, Mormon doctrine was the Swiss Army Knife of mystical knowledge. For example, you might wonder if people in the Celestial Kingdom (the top heavenly prize) could visit the poor souls suffering their everlasting lives' away in the Terrestrial and Telestial Kingdoms. The answer happened to be yes; Celestial Saints could visit the sinners, but they couldn't visit us—it's was a one-way ticket. I supposed it was like visiting a family member in prison. It was also the sort of thing that most Gentiles just didn't know. On a bright note, even the cellar-dwelling Telestial Kingdom wasn't supposed to be that bad. In fact, Joseph Smith said if we knew how good even the Telestial Kingdom was in comparison to this earth, we'd kill ourselves to go there.

Knowing all the heavenly mysteries gave us peace of mind (at least I know it gave me comfort, just knowing everything like I did).

My Grandma West always said that things happened for a reason. What she meant, I supposed, was that a Grand Puppeteer hovered above us, directing every event, large and small. But I didn't necessarily buy that. Even as an adolescent boy, I didn't think we needed to know everything, and it didn't make sense to me that every event had to *mean* something. I could accept that some things just happened off script. And if there was an omnipotent puppeteer, it seemed like his moves came off poorly choreographed at times.

I wasn't an especially contemplative boy, but I often wondered where God was when we needed him the most.

Why didn't he intervene with worldwide heartache, famine, and genocide? I saw pictures of starving children in Africa with flies in their eyes. Where was God, I wondered? There were times I didn't like him very much for refusing to step in. I could never understand how he'd allow bad things to happen even to prayerful Mormons who appeared to keep the commandments down to the dotted i. And, of course, there was the fact that he sat back while good things happened to bad people, horrible people really. Maybe there was a plan. Maybe it would all come out in the end and the rotten apples would finally get their comeuppance—especially Rocky Hollingsworth who backed over my bike in his brand-new Camaro without saying a word, like I wouldn't notice.

I did see evidence, at times, of the master plan—of the Grand Puppeteer. For example, take the time I went on a road trip with my high school friend, Spence, when I was almost 18.

We left Salt Lake City with a general plan to "go to California". My parents were laissez-faire about the whole thing. I told them we'd be gone for about three weeks. Fine. Be careful, they said. Remember who you are, they said. That was a favorite mantra of my mom: "Remember who you are and what you stand for." In fact, it was probably her primary go-to, but she also had others, including the popular classic: "Evil prevails when good men do nothing." That's why she boycotted *Young Frankenstein* and *Jesus Christ Superstar*. (Although she appeared to enjoy *Chitty Chitty Bang Bang*.)

We roamed around San Francisco for a week, then Los Angeles, and finally down the coast to San Diego. I was sleeping on the sofa of the friend of a friend's cousin when I had the most vivid dream. Spence and I were lying on the paved road. We were in the desert and it was dark. Spence's light-blue VW bug was off the road and tipped on its side. I could make out red flashing lights, round and round, like a police car or an ambulance was nearby. I turned my head and looked at Spence just as paramedics were pulling a white sheet over his head. It was so real.

I woke, freaked out, and sat up from the sofa. It was about four o'clock in the morning. Right then, the phone rang. Everyone in the house was asleep, passed out really, so I grabbed it on the second ring. I *knew* it was going to be my mom on the other end of the line. I can't explain how or why I knew, because my mom didn't even know where we were other than in California somewhere, and she was loath to make long-distance calls because of the cost.

"Oh, Warren," she said. "I'm so glad you answered." There was enormous relief in her voice. "I had the most terrible dream," she said. "I woke your dad up two hours ago and we've been calling everyone we know, trying to track you down." Wow, that's pretty weird, I thought. "I dreamed you were driving home at night, in the desert, and you had an accident. I dreamed that you were lying on the pavement and the ambulance was there. They were pulling a white sheet over you. I needed to reach you. I needed to make sure you were okay. I don't know why, but it was such a vivid dream and I couldn't sleep until I reached you."

What did this mean? At the very least my mom and I were on the same wavelength. But what else? My mom believed it was a religious experience, that God was somehow communicating to us through our dreams to warn us of impending doom. Maybe so, but if he didn't want me to get in an accident, why would he fuss with the dreams and phone calls? Why not just nudge Spence to keep him awake at the wheel? And why didn't he warn everybody? Hey, Phil, you might want to watch out for that dump truck next Saturday. I didn't ask my mom those questions, and upon my safe return (we drove home during daylight hours, not a mile over the speed limit in the slow lane, with seatbelts and pillows on our laps, hoping to jinx the dream) she bore her testimony to me that this was unimpeachable evidence that the church was true.

As for myself, I didn't know what to make of it. Did our coincident dreams mean the golden tablets were real? I didn't know, but it had to mean *something*. Didn't it?

And that wasn't the only incident that made me wonder. Here's another one. Our Boy Scout troop went on a float trip down the Yampa River. There were about five rubber boats loaded with five or six boys each, plus our supplies and one or two adult supervisors (one of whom knew very little about white-water rafting). We successfully negotiated our way through hairy rapids like Little Joe's and Greasy Pliers. (When I say successfully, I mean to say that only a few boys fell out and they were pulled back into the boats before they drowned. "Dude, you went flyin'!") But on Day Three we were expected to hit the biggies, including Teepee and the granddaddy of them all, the Warm Springs rapids.

Danny, Roger, and Kent were all riding with a dimwit adult who was supposed to know what he was doing. He plainly did not. The rest of our boats had successfully made it through Warm Springs, all of us hanging on for dear life, screaming, soaked, and nearly capsizing. But the boat Danny was riding in wasn't so lucky. It got pinned against a huge boulder in the middle of the river, the 10-foot-tall rapids smashing around the rock in violent swells and waves. The boat took on water and flipped upside down. Danny, Roger, and the adult captain floated down the river and were pulled to safety about 200 yards downstream (along with their drenched sleeping bags and Coleman coolers of food). Kent, however, had hung on to the rock somehow and scampered on top of it before the boat flipped. He now stood atop this rock in the middle of the torrent, some 15 feet above water. Below and all around him were huge, life-threatening rapids.

We walked back upstream and stood on the bank adjacent to Kent, stranded on that enormous boulder. The river was maybe 40 yards wide at that point and he was right in the middle of it, 20 yards from shore. The adults huddled. What were we going to do? We couldn't get to him with a boat, and we certainly couldn't swim to him. He was stuck. There was only one way out of this: Kent would have to jump into the rapids with his life jacket and just hope he didn't drown.

We all gathered to pray on the side of the bank. After additional private prayers were said, the scout leaders, including my dad, yelled to Kent to advise him what he must do. They had to cup their hands around their mouths and yell as loud as they could over the thundering sound of the river. Kent took this news like a man. There was only the somber nod of his head. We all held our breath as he approached the edge of the boulder, almost jumped, then stepped back to collect his final thoughts. I was just happy it wasn't me up there.

He stood on the edge and counted down: Five, Four, Three, Two, One. Then he jumped. We didn't see him for about five seconds as he was violently pulled beneath the surface, churning like a rag doll through the coils of water. Just when I thought he was done for, he popped up about 40 yards downstream. I will never forget his heroic gesture when he appeared and started bobbing down the mellower current. He held both hands high above his head and flashed the peace sign like Richard Nixon used to do. We cheered.

That evening we had an impromptu testimony meeting around the campfire. Everyone offered solemn witness that God had saved the day because of our prayers. I had to agree, even though there was the initial thought that if God hadn't wanted Kent to be harmed, he could have helped steer the damned boat away from the rock in the first place. But they said, oh no, this had been a test, carefully orchestrated by God, to see what we'd do. That's the way he operates. He allows us to put ourselves in a pickle and then, if we prayerfully ask him to save us, he might. Sometimes. And sometimes not, for his will is mysterious. But that time he did.

It was also a test of faith. Kent didn't want to jump, of course he didn't, but he trusted the priesthood leaders and took a literal leap of faith. He passed with flying colors and God saved him because of it. (I happened to have firsthand knowledge, however, that he hadn't been saved because of his unblemished record of virtue, for he was a miscreant like the rest of us.)

The entire event was all quite faith-promoting as it was, but even more so when my dad reported that he'd had a dream vision the night before. In that vision he'd seen this very event play out, right down to the rock, the flipped boat, and the leap. When he woke up that morning, he'd tried to reorganize the boat captains or otherwise switch it up to counteract the vision, so it wouldn't play out. But the other adult leaders had resisted. "Don't worry about it, Leonard," they'd said. "We weren't born yesterday—we'll be careful," they'd said. We all listened to my dad later that night with a mixture of awe and wonder (the adults he'd forewarned were rather sheepish and didn't say much, and tried to act busy by putting another stick on the fire). My dad had seen it all play out beforehand! This was confirmation that God really was involved.

I assumed God paid extra attention to us because we were his Chosen People. Consequently, I assumed our prayers had more oomph than other people's. I couldn't prove it but it seemed that way to me. Either way, the lesson to be learned from the rafting mishap was simply this: When God told us something, it was wise to sit up and listen, especially if he was speaking through my dad.

13

I WAS GIVEN A BOOK OF REMEMBRANCE for my 11th birthday. That was a book with a number of pages that basically looked like empty March Madness brackets. We used the brackets to fill in our ancestral line back as far as we could go. Ideally, you'd go all the way back to Adam and Eve, but nobody had been able to do that yet. Usually they'd get bogged down by the time they got to their great-great grandparents (and maybe their great-great-*great* grandparents). That's what happened to me. I was gung-ho for a while, doing my genealogy like it was going out of style, hunkered down over the kitchen table with a pencil and eraser, concentrating with my tongue poking out, copying my dad's line of ancestors with names like Uriah and Shadrach. Then I ran out of steam.

There were some thumbnail black and white photos of my ancestors. This was sobering. I knew I shouldn't judge, especially since I was part of the downline, but my ancestors didn't look like the pick of the litter. They were pioneer stock and looked it. Notwithstanding the fact that they were the Chosen People, nowhere were the good tidings evident on their faces, which looked like they'd been exposed to too much sun, wind, and dirt. And it was universally clear they'd all been given bad hair advice.

Mormons were always big on genealogy. Real big. I'll tell you why: It's so they can baptize their long-lost ancestors into the true church. People sometimes wonder how you can baptize someone who's already dead. That was a conundrum that perplexed Joseph Smith for some time, in fact, until he finally received a revelation explaining it.

As I and everyone else knew, you had to be baptized before you were allowed into heaven. This fact was common knowledge. But it had to be a *proper* baptism or it wouldn't take. I was taught that only a Mormon baptism would do the trick, because the most famous baptizer in human history, none other than John the Baptist, personally came down from heaven to show Joseph Smith how to do it. And no other church could claim that.

Like all Mormons, I got baptized when I was 8 years old, for that is the age when you should be old enough to know right from wrong and be held accountable for your sinning. It's also the age at which you can affirmatively choose to get baptized, so it's not foisted upon you. I didn't know where they came up with that number. Eight? Even then it seemed pretty young to be weighing the merits of such a profound decision when your salvation teetered in the balance. "So, Warren, do you want to get baptized?" Yeah, I guess. "Are you choosing this voluntarily?" Uh, what does voluntary mean? "Well, have you considered the doctrines of the church and do you wish to be baptized for the remission of your sins by your own accord?" What's a remission accord? But I was like every other 8-year old in the 200-year history of the church; I wasn't about to defer my baptism against my parents' wishes. "Nope, you know what mom and dad? The more I think about it, I just don't feel ready. I need to study more of the doctrine."

Baptism was supposed to wash away our sins. For that reason, I was always jealous of those people who were baptized later in their life. I felt gypped, because those people just sinned their lives away—eating, drinking, and being merry and then they got baptized and were washed clean as a whistle. This did not seem fair to me. Besides, how many sins could I have accumulated by the time I was 8? It seemed like a total waste of a complete cleansing. I didn't even like the smell of coffee when I was 8. Okay, maybe I'd jaywalked, but I hadn't even learned a legitimate swear word by then. The good news was I could repent later in life, which had the same basic effect of baptism, but I still thought it was a disadvantage to do it so early. I should have at least waited through my high school years.

I was also bestowed with the Gift of the Holy Ghost after I was baptized. I would have preferred a gift I could unwrap, like a new pair of Adidas baseball cleats, but this gift was the promise that the Holy Ghost would accompany me wherever I went from that time forth, to keep me on track and to provide comfort. Of course, I couldn't see him because he was invisible, as I figured any normal ghost would be. I imagined him trailing a few feet behind and slightly above me, sort of like Casper, but holier. Most of the time I forgot he was by my side but I figured he kept me on the straight and narrow as best he could.

Baptism in my religion was by immersion. Complete immersion. None of this sprinkling business. Therefore, I actually had to get baptized twice because the first time the tip of my big toe popped up out of the water. My dad, who was the one baptizing me, had to redo it from scratch. (Anyone with the priesthood is allowed to perform a baptism.) So, technically, I was baptized twice. I knew complete immersion meant complete immersion, and I didn't wish to nitpick with Mormon doctrine back then, but I wasn't so sure it had to be done that second time. I was confident the tip of my toe was not riddled with sin. Even going forward I assumed my toe would mostly stay out of trouble.

Baptizing dead people solved the question of what to do about our ancestors who lived before the true church was established in 1830. They obviously hadn't been properly baptized because they lived before Joseph Smith came along, so they couldn't go to heaven. There was much hand wringing over this dilemma. What would happen to these people? Was it fair they were denied entrance to heaven just because they happened to die before 1830? Were the Aztecs and Incas basically screwed? Were the Vikings simply SOL?

No, they weren't. And they could thank the Mormons for enabling their salvation. The practical solution was to take a living person, pretend he was a dead person, and then baptize him posthumously. This was serious business, baptizing dead people.

Some of my best memories as a boy were getting "Baptized for the Dead." Our whole Sunday School class would go to the Mormon temple in downtown Salt Lake City and dress in white clothes. Then, one by one, we'd be led into the baptismal font where the warm water came up to our waist. A Mormon man with the proper priesthood authority would read the name of a dead person that had been supplied to him by someone's genealogy homework, then dunk us in the water. We'd come up for air and he would read another dead person's name and dunk us again. It was like getting dunked in a hot tub by your big brother, again and again, only with reverent intent. We'd be baptized maybe 10 times before it was another boy's turn. Then we'd get out, dry off, and wait for our buddy to get baptized for another 10 people, and so on.

I can't remember whose identity I took. I might have been Guillermo Valdez from the 18th century for 10 seconds and then I'd be Chiang Zhang Wei from the Middle Ages for the next 10 seconds. My buddies might have been, say, Alexander the Great, or a long-lost, dead uncle. Meanwhile the dead person's spirit was watching all this from the spirit world and, if he accepted the baptism, he would then be admitted into heaven. It wasn't compulsory; if the dead person's spirit didn't accept the baptism, then so be it. No one could force someone to become a Mormon, not even God.

Anyway, that was the reason for collecting all the names in Mormon genealogy centers, so all those dead people could be baptized properly. Once they'd gone through the low-hanging fruit, the ancestors they knew about, then they'd move on to anyone who had ever lived, giving as many dead people as possible the chance to go to heaven.

There was a mad rush to save the celebrities. I mean, who wouldn't want to be Clark Gable for ten seconds? It gives the Saints no small comfort (and no small amount of pride) to know that Christopher Columbus was baptized Mormon, as were George and Martha Washington. Frank Sinatra has been baptized a Mormon now, too. I heard they also baptized Adolph Hitler and the Boston Strangler, which was charitable, since probably no other church would've taken them. They didn't need to baptize Ted Bundy after he was executed because he was already a Mormon.

After we'd all been baptized about a dozen times, our Sunday School teacher would take us to Snelgrove's for ice cream. It was a lot of fun.

————————

I went to General Conference twice a year with my family. It was basically the Mormon equivalent of Hajj. Conference was held in the Tabernacle, a domed meeting hall that could seat about 7,000 Saints and sits next to the main Temple in Salt Lake City, in Temple Square. Maybe you've seen photos of it with the Mormon Tabernacle Choir sitting in front, color coordinated. It was tough to get in because there were too many Mormons for such few seats. I could get in whenever I wanted because my dad was an usher, but I never really *wanted* to get in. It was basically a really long church service. I marveled that adults would stand in line for hours in the cold and rain, hoping for a seat.

The conferences were boring, listening to old white men drone on about subjects I really didn't care about; things like the atonement and chastity, punctuated every half hour by the choir singing *I Stand All Amazed* or *The Battle Hymn of the Republic*. The pews were wooden, with no padding whatsoever, and they'd been built 150 years before the advent of fast-food when people were skinnier, so we were squished in, knee to knee.

My dad was a man of many talents and one of them was being able to sleep standing up (or on his stomach on the floor, on top of *Blondie* and *Beetle Bailey* with five kids crawling all over him on Sunday afternoons). I'd see him standing there in an aisle on the balcony and I knew he was dead asleep. I could just tell. Once, after the service (and we had to stay for at least an hour after until everyone cleared out), my dad took us up into the attic. It was one of the coolest things I'd ever seen. The wooden beams were huge and they were all held together by strips of leather. They hadn't even used nails in the construction of that huge building. Once the beams were in place, they'd dunk a strip of tanned hide into water and let it get good and soaked, then wrap the strip around the two beams. As the leather dried it would shrink, binding the wood together as good as a nail. This, to an 8-year-old boy, proved beyond a shadow of a doubt the church was true.

The Tabernacle was also known for its impressive acoustics. I heard one time about a devout, elderly soul from southern Utah who took a tour of the place. To demonstrate the acoustics, the tour guide said, "I will now show you how incredible the acoustics are. Please stand at the rear of the building and I will drop a pin on the pulpit and I'll bet you will hear the pin drop." The tour guide then dropped the pin on the pulpit, and the elderly man's eyes became misty and he choked up. He gravely said, "If that don't prove the church is true, why, I don't know what does."

14

MY WIFE'S BEST FRIEND GROWING UP WAS Mary Jane, who happens to be my cousin. I think I have 82 cousins. In fact, it was Mary Jane who lined us up for our first date. Cindy was wary about going out with me because she had grown up around Mary Jane who'd told her harrowing tales about her cousins' poverty. It turns out the Driggs's were the destitute cousins she had been referring to. I'm not sure why she had such a notable impression of our pecuniary situation. Was it because we had no TV? Or that we had no dishwasher and a lawn mower without an engine? Or was it because we'd arrive for a visit in our old, packed station wagon with the faux-wood paneling on the side, disembarking one at a time like those Russian stacking dolls? Or was it our mismatched hand-me-down clothes?

We weren't *poor* poor. There was always plenty to eat and we lived in a middle-class neighborhood. I may have mentioned that my dad was an auto mechanic when I was born. He worked hard, too. I didn't know anyone who valued hard work as much as my dad. It was a central ethic in his life. Of the Seven Deadly Sins, he'd barely register on the sloth barometer (same thing with envy and greed—they weren't his thing either). When he was older and you'd ask him what he'd been up to, he'd apologize for his sloth. "Oh, just being lazy," he'd say, as if there was a moral demerit in sitting a few hours to watch *Matlock*.

When my grandfather died, my 7-year-old dad figured he had to become the family breadwinner. He sold newspapers on the corner of Main Street. His biggest haul was the day the Salt Lake Tribune's headline read in bold letters: **JAPAN DECLARES WAR, BLASTS U.S. IN THE PACIFIC. FDR Slates Address This Morning**. He was so young he could barely read it. My dad's reading level stayed low his entire life. And his spelling? Two examples: Woran and the Quonsert Quire.

Hard work trumped education for my dad. In fact, he was never big on getting anything more than a high school diploma. He thought I'd be better off "getting a leg up" by starting a career in sales directly out of high school. My mom was more conflicted. She put more value on formal education even though she didn't graduate high school. However, she was concerned about what higher education might try to brainwash us with. She figured (quite rightly as it turned out) that college professors would expose us to the world and the liberal debauchery that came with it, including vices like biology, anthropology, and evolution—ideas which would work like a nutcracker on our comfy cocoons.

My dad was a natural born salesman. One of a kind. Charismatic, honest, and extremely likable. He'd give the money from his newspaper sales to my grandmother, a 43-year-old widow with six children. They'd been poor before my grandfather died, but afterwards they were on the very margin of survival.

A few weeks after graduating high school, my dad got married and bought a Mobil station off West Temple Street in Salt Lake

City. He was an incredibly hard worker and gifted salesman, but a lousy businessman. He was also unusually gullible with a nature that bordered on complete naivete—a wholesale surrender to the goodness of mankind. His employees knew this and robbed him on a regular basis. It wasn't hard to do. Most transactions were done in cash back then. An employee would fill a customer's gas tank and be paid the two dollars in cash, which he'd slip into his pocket, easy as pie.

So my dad was an easy mark. I don't know how many times over the years he'd remind me that he probably owed me money for jobs I'd done, when I knew I hadn't done squat. I often took the money, too, setting aside any questions about whether or not I deserved it.

He eventually lost all his investment, and Mobil took the gas station away from him when I was about 5. He owed everyone, including his suppliers and the very employees who'd stolen from him. That's when a customer named Joe Winder offered him a job selling insurance. Joe was a decent, honest, immaculate man who saw something special in my dad. He could see that this grease monkey with the pompadour hairstyle and bright blue eyes had no fancy polish but was so *likeable*.

My mom was mortified that my dad would be an insurance salesman. This, at the time, was a lower-rung job than owning a gas station. She worried that he'd hit up all the neighbors and family members for their insurance business—that they'd dodge and duck whenever they'd see him coming, afraid he'd shake them down for a life insurance policy. She made him promise he'd never ask anyone they knew to buy insurance. It was a promise he would keep.

My dad began his career with State Farm Insurance when I was about 6-years-old. He scheduled appointments late into the night, trying to make ends meet and trying to repay the debts from the gas station. People suggested he declare bankruptcy, but that would have been anathema to my dad. His personal honor code would allow for no such thing. He would pay every single debt. The appearance of our poverty during my adolescent years wasn't due to inadequate income, but rather the fact that so much of my dad's earnings were used to pay off his debts. It took him until I was a teenager, pecking away at it, but he made good on every cent.

My parents were obviously busy during this period in their lives. There were the industrial-sized loads of wash and wiping snotty noses, chores which were not the sole province of my mom. You see, my dad wasn't like most men at the time who'd sit with their arms folded, waiting for dinner to be served. Not my dad. He was a modern man who'd been plopped into the 1960's. He did most of the food shopping and his share of the dishes, cleaning, diaper changing, and cooking. My wife said she wanted to marry me because of my dad.

A few years after my dad got started in the insurance business, it became law that all cars be insured. That was his career break. He sold a few policies, and then a few more. The story of Leonard Driggs became a legendary one, for by the time I was 25-years-old, my dad, the one who could barely read, the one who could barely spell, the one who had barely graduated high school, had become the largest volume State Farm insurance agent in the world. *Number One* out of nearly 20,000 agents.

My dad wasn't very interested in the money, but he was not immune to pride. I remember as a boy the way he'd bring home the lists of agents and where he ranked among them in Utah and around the country. My mom called these his "brag sheets" and they showed an impressive climb up the ladder. Sometimes they'd be taped to the fridge. There were all those policies he'd sold, sales contests he'd won, and incentive trips he'd earned.

When I was 18, my parents took me to Hawaii on one of those trips. The welcome dinner was a luau on the beach where they were roasting a pig. I'd never seen a pig on a spit and it sort of grossed me out. I mean, it was the whole danged pig, its four stiff legs flung out in a cry for help. My parents, leis around their necks, were sitting at the head table with the president of State Farm, a man named Ed Rust. His status and position had everyone at the table kowtowing. Well, everyone except my mom. She asked Mr. Rust if he'd ever been on Oprah. When he said he hadn't, my mom said, "Well, then I guess you're not *that* big of a deal." Everyone at the table erupted with laughter, including Mr. Rust.

I was stuck at a different table with some insurance agents from North Carolina. These adults had no use for me, of course, some teenage kid with hair down to his shoulders and a puka-shell necklace. But when we went around the table introducing ourselves and I said my name was Warren Rust, the adults stopped mid-bite, like one of those old EF Hutton commercials. "Rust, did you say?" Yeah. Suddenly they were interested. "Do you happen to know Mr. Ed Rust?" Yeah, that's my dad, I said. You would've thought I'd just won the Kentucky Derby the way they started fawning all over me. Here, have another roll! Want more butter? Can we get you another dessert? Luckily, Mr. Rust was a good sport when he found out about my little ruse, but he must have wondered about Leonard Driggs's wife and son.

When my dad had extra money, he gave it away to any organization or person in need. When he didn't have it, he'd go to the bank and borrow it so he could give it away. Maybe it was his childhood poverty that made him want to help other people, but he had an interesting relationship with money. He demonstrated this the time he bought a hat in Mexico. We were at a beach, and a Mexican salesman with a tall stack of sombreros walked by, hawking his wares to the Gringos. This is how it went:

"Hey, amigo, you want buy sombrero?"

"How much?" my dad asked.

"20 pesos."

"Hmmm," my dad said. "I'll pay you 25 pesos."

"15 pesos," said the Mexican salesman.

"I'll pay 40," said my dad.

"Okay, you pay 8 pesos?"

"No," said my dad. "I'll pay 50."

On it went until the salesman dropped his asking price to 5 pesos and my dad was up to 100, where finally the deal was struck. One hundred pesos for the sombrero. The Mexican man took the money, looked my dad over like he was the craziest sonofabitch he'd ever done business with, and walked away down the beach. My dad never said a thing to us kids. There was no lecture on charity, and certainly not one on bargaining strategy. Every time I saw my dad wearing that stupid sombrero, I was reminded of what he cared about, and didn't care about.

Even though my dad didn't appear to care about money, he did like coins. He was an avid coin collector. He'd come home with bags of pennies and dump them out on the kitchen table and we'd all sort them, plugging them into our little blue coin-collecting books according to year and mint. After my parents passed away, we were cleaning out their house to sell it. Remember those damned 50-gallon drums of wheat in the basement? Well, we also found a few secret hiding spots with bags of silver dollars (one was on the top shelf of the linen closet behind a stack of old pillow cases that hadn't been used in 30 years). I have no clue what prompted him to hide them. Maybe he was saving them for the Last Days when the only currency would be gold or silver. I figured it wouldn't have been easy lugging all that silver to the Garden of Eden in Jackson County, Missouri. On the other hand, if someone had asked him to give them the coins, he probably would have.

I spent three hours looking for more loot after we discovered the silver dollars in the linen closet. I searched for fake doors and any drawers with possible secret compartments. I tapped the sheetrock listening for hollow spaces. I found nothing.

After my dad passed away, three separate people, who presumably didn't know each other, approached me with similar stories. I didn't know any of these people, had never heard of them in fact. They had been my dad's policyholders but had each encountered financial hardship at some point and hadn't been able to pay their insurance premiums. A year after they quit paying their premiums (and two years for one guy), they had a loss and called my dad, lamenting the fact that they weren't still covered. My dad told them that in fact they were. "But, how, Leonard? I haven't paid my premiums in over a year!" "I know," replied my dad. "I knew you were having a hard time, so I've been paying them for you."

My siblings all have stories along those same lines.

I have no idea how much money my dad gave away. Often times they were "loans" without any realistic expectation of repayment, because he didn't want to make people feel like they were the subjects of charity. My brother, Danny, was the executor of my parent's estate. Shortly before he died, my dad gave Danny a book (like a ledger) which listed the names of literally hundreds of people my dad had loaned money to. He instructed Danny to accept repayment from these people if offered. Not a single one did. They spoke glowingly of their love and admiration for my dad, but no one put their money where their mouth was.

My parents drummed into us that we should be givers, not takers, and that there was always a scale to measure it by. In fact, my mom used to say there were only two kinds of people in the world; the ones who walked into a room and said "Here I am!" and the ones who walked into a room and said "There you are!" My parents were "There You Are" kind of people to a T.

My dad a year before he died. Of all the photos that capture my dad, this is probably it.

My first photo

My dad began his career with State Farm after he lost his Mobil gas station. He would become the largest volume agent in America.

Me and my dad shortly before he passed away.

Little League All Stars. Danny is the first one on the bottom row from the left and I am sitting next to him

The Pennant

My mom

First day of school. From left: Ben, Paul, Jane, Dave, me, and Danny.
Missing Julie, Steve, Matt, and Andy.

13th "B" day

Birthday cake my dad and I made for my 13th birthday. My mom was in the hospital giving birth to my eighth sibling, Steve.

Only missing my youngest sibling, Andy.

Practicing for my career as a tightrope walker, a career that petered out fairly quickly.

One of our first high school dates.

My cousins on my mom's side of the family. I am in the middle, in front of my dad. I have this many more cousins on my dad's side, too.

At the airport when I returned from my mission.
Danny is holding Steve and I am holding Andy.

15

I HAVE A FAIRLY STRONG WORK ETHIC and I credit my dad for that, but my mom was no slouch either. She made us work. We had our dishwashing day, our gardens to weed, and our lawn to mow with a push mower. I thought this was the height of cruelty because all my other friends had gas powered mowers. Heck, those looked *fun*. I'd gladly have mowed the lawn with one of those, probably even agree to mow a few strips of the neighbor's lawn, too. But my parents said it was good exercise, as if I needed to shed some weight from my 70-pound frame.

You are undoubtedly aware of the Lonestar State, the Sunshine State, and the Show-me State. But for those who don't know, Utah is the Beehive State. The beehive is a symbol of hard work and industry, for we here in Utah are industrious little bees, buzzing around with hardly any evidence of sloth. There is a large beehive on our state flag to prove it, but I think a handsome embroidery of my parents would have represented the work ethic just as effectively.

My mom was different than moms of today—you know, the moms who hover. I didn't see her until after school because she was usually in bed with a headache in the mornings. My dad woke us up with his daily refrain: "Good morning, merry sunshine, how did you wake so soon? You used to wake at nine o'clock and now you wake at noon!" He'd fix a pot of mush for our breakfast, or milk toast, and no—my mother was not there hovering. In fact, I could have grown a handlebar mustache in the second grade and I doubt either of my parents would have noticed. I had tree huts and underground caves that could have easily collapsed and buried me alive and my mom wouldn't have known where to start her search when I didn't come home by the time it was dark. "Hmph, it seems like I haven't seen Warren in a while. You?" At least I was in our own backyard when I decided I might have a future as a tightrope walker. I spent hours walking the top bar of our rickety swing set, a death-defying act without a safety net. My mom didn't even remind me to be careful. I supposed she didn't want me to fall any more than I did.

My first jobs were helping my dad at his office. I swept the floors and filled the coke machine, things I thought made me indispensable. But, on the chance these were make-work projects to get me out of the house and give my mom a break, I'd have to pronounce my first official employment as a door-to-door salesman. I was 9 or 10 years-old and my specialty was selling light bulbs. I didn't sell light bulbs for something to do, the way some kids set up lemonade stands. I did it for the money.

My dad would go to the Westinghouse warehouse and come home with the station wagon full of light bulbs. We divided them amongst us kids in the living room, picked neighborhoods, and took off, going door to door with 25-watt, 60-watt, 75-watt, and 100-watt bulbs. We carried them in home-made boxes with straps around our necks. I sold the bulbs for about a quarter each. Believe me, please, when I say I knocked on virtually every door within a five-mile radius of my house wearing my discount tennis shoes. I could tell that some customers bought out of sheer pity. On the other hand, who couldn't use at least one light bulb?

We sold candles or factory-damaged dolls when the light bulbs ran out. I didn't think selling was a hardship. In fact, there were times it was a lot of fun. And the thrill of making a sale? Priceless, especially if a neighbor went all in on a three-way bulb that cost twice as much. I'll never forget when Mike Coombs's mom bought my entire box for $15.75.

I presume our poor neighbors could see us coming: "Oh my, Gilbert, look, it's the Driggs kids again. They're selling Christmas candles," she'd say as she stood with her hands on her hips looking out the picture window of their living room. "But, Betty, it's the middle of June! Weren't they just here last week trying to sell us light bulbs?"

When it was too far to walk, my dad would drop me off in a neighborhood and pick me up at a designated time (if he remembered). I was never lost because I could track my bearings by the north-south Wasatch mountains bordering Salt Lake City, a wall of impenetrable comfort and safety. And Mt. Olympus, front and center, stood guard over our community, a gigantic granite sentinel. An iconic, immovable marker of home.

Rain, sleet, unbearable summer heat, it didn't matter, for I was a good little capitalist. We'd come back to our home office with stories from the road (rabid dogs, doors slammed, people in their underwear), comparing our wads of cash like we'd do with our Halloween hauls after Trick or Treating. After we reimbursed our dad for the wholesale cost of the goods (which he underestimated to the extreme), we'd pocket the rest. I could make $20 on a good day. Not too shabby for a 10-year old.

Twenty dollars would've been the gross, but then I owed tithing. Mormons, even 10-year olds, were supposed to pay the church 10% of everything they earned. I was never a whiz at math (I still can't subtract if I need to carry) but this was painful. Maybe that was the whole point; that it wasn't about the money, per se, but rather God's strategy to make us sacrifice as proof that we loved him.

It only took me a few tithing payments to understand why the Mormon church was one of the wealthiest institutions in America. I didn't feel cynical about a system that tied my salvation to my wallet, because I knew the church did a lot of good things with the money. I heard different stories when I was growing up about the Mormon welfare system and all that went on down at Welfare Square. I gradually learned that Mormons not only took care of their own, but helped with humanitarian needs around the world, shipping containers of food and emergency supplies east, west, north, and south.

I didn't stress over whether I should pay my tithing on the gross or the net because I didn't really pay taxes back then. But I heard plenty of talk about it. "You do what your conscience tells you," the bishop advised, which I thought was code for quit being a cheapskate. Most people thought it wise to pay it on the gross. Why go nickel and diming the Lord when the Celestial Kingdom hangs in the balance? Why voluntarily pave your own way to the Terrestrial? God sees everything, they said. He's good at math, they said. But I was torn because I liked the money, too. I didn't want to be like the Amish with their carriages and a single change of homemade clothes.

The Prophet relayed a promise from God that if Mormons paid a full tithing, even if they were broke, he'd reward them. And it wasn't just the mouth-watering reward of heaven, but prosperity here on earth, too. I don't know how many faith-promoting stories I heard in church over the bounties you'd receive by paying a full tithing. "Why, Melva had herself a terrible bladder infection but we paid our tithing and it went away two weeks later!" Or, maybe it would be something like this: "Earl got fired from his job but we paid our tithing anyway and I'll be darned if he didn't get a new one the next week!" I didn't know what a bladder infection was, but I got the point. And the point was this: The windows of heaven were opening and God was leaning out, looking down on us from heaven with a twinkle in his eye. Away to the window he'd fly like a flash, tear open the shutters and throw down the cash!

I don't wish to rat out the IRS, but a tax attorney once told me the IRS doesn't flip out over excessive charitable deductions on a tax return with a Utah zip code. The principal reason for that is the ubiquity of tithing—ten percent of all earnings, which is nothing to sneeze at. And if Mormons were somehow able to monetize their time spent in service projects, they wouldn't owe any taxes at all.

As a Mormon wage earner, I had to go to Tithing Settlement at the end of every year, where I met privately with the bishop in his office at the ward house to make sure my tithing ledgers were up to snuff. I remember sitting there in a leather wingback across from the bishop's executive desk. On the credenza behind him was an 8 x 10 photo of his wife and six children and another one of the current president (the president of the church—this wasn't like the post office). I shook like a leaf when he asked me, point blank, if I was a full tithe payer. I thought I was, but I couldn't be 100% sure. Maybe my dad had given me a few dollars for sweeping the office and I'd blown it on a candy bar. And I knew the bishop would know if I was lying. He just would. Bishops had their ways. Besides that, there was a mirror in his office and I thought it might have been one of those two-way jobs and Jesus was on the other side checking out my story and taking notes. (I didn't really believe this. A two-way mirror? Come on. But I did think of it.)

I'd come out of the meeting with the bishop with sweat coating my palms, my parents waiting with satisfied smiles. It gave me no small amount of comfort to know I was pre-paying my lease on the Celestial Kingdom.

I used most of my work money for clothes. My first purchase was a three-pack of boxer shorts, because I'd been at Bruce Jones's house for a sleepover with a few other buddies and I was the only kid wearing tighty-whities. The next day I pedaled my bike to Grand Central (our supermarket) and bought the plaid three-pack. I couldn't wait for the next sleepover. Heck, I was so proud of them, I would have worn them to school with no pants. I presume my mom found out about my upgraded underwear when she found them in the dirty clothes bin. She never mentioned it.

My second purchase was a pair of jeans that all the popular kids wore. My mom couldn't understand why I would spend such an outrageous sum on the pair with the tiny label on the back pocket. Obviously, it was the label that made them cool. Just ask Brad Jorgenson. But she still tried to talk me out of it. "I know you really want them, but this pair will last just as long." Well, I know that, mom. I knew she didn't want me to be unpopular, and was only trying to save me some money, but I didn't trust her taste. I thought she and my dad had about as much fashion sense as the American Gothic couple.

But my most expensive purchase was a Wilson A-2000 baseball mitt. It cost $50 and was made from heavy leather. I slept with that mitt under my pillow with a baseball inside the pocket of the glove to form it. This left a crick in my neck and my bedroom smelled like linseed oil because I kept rubbing it on the mitt to soften up the leather. Of all the purchases in my life, that is the most memorable one. More memorable than a car or a house.

I supplemented my door-to-door employment with a number of other jobs ranging from snow shoveling to yardwork. I was nearly old enough to drive by the time I landed a job at Lagoon, the largest amusement park in Utah. That was a sweet job. I started out as a sweeper, walking up and down the main corridors dressed in my official uniform with a small broom and dust pan. I swept up cigarette butts and cotton candy tubes.

My first philosophical challenge beset me when I was in front of the Rock-O-Plane sweeping up a discarded ticket. I assumed the person who'd dropped it was an unrepentant litterbug. I swept for a few moments more, wondering if I would be a litterbug if I returned that ticket to the pavement. I was no Voltaire, but this vexing philosophical question kept me intrigued for an hour. Would that make me a litterbug, too? I'd picked it up in the first place, which was the opposite of littering, and I'd just be moving the piece of litter from one spot to another. I ultimately concluded that I would be litter-neutral. I also wondered why birds didn't get electrocuted when they perched on a powerline, and why it wasn't always windy if the earth was spinning in circles through space. Those were the weighty conundrums that occupied my time as I swept, hour after hour, watching girls with halter tops and spoiled kids walking around with snow cones in one hand and a stuffed teddy bear head-locked in the other arm.

I swept for a summer and was then promoted to game operator. I ran the game where a customer tries to ring the bell with a sledge hammer. I worked on commission and made a fortune (like, $5.00 an hour). It was like taking candy from a baby when I'd see a tough guy strolling down the midway, just as macho as he could be. Hey, Tough Guy, ring the bell and win a stuffed animal for your pretty girlfriend. They'd spend 20 bucks trying to win a two-dollar stuffed panda. Some of them became mad at me because they said it was rigged. It wasn't, and they must've felt pretty sheepish when the next guy handed over his five stuffed animals to his wife, grabbed the sledgehammer, and rang it again. I became a fearless salesman between my job at Lagoon and my door-to-door light bulb sales.

I also had the newspaper route in the seventh grade. This was not a good job. I had to wake up at five o'clock in the morning and pedal my bike a mile and a half to the newspaper drop area, load the newspapers into the wire basket mounted to the handlebars of my 40-pound Red Flyer, and then pedal around the neighborhood delivering them. It was dark and usually freezing cold. I'd get back to my house by six-thirty and then get ready for school. I did it every morning.

Throwing the papers to the porches of individual homes was easy but, unfortunately, I also had a nursing home on my route. I think it might have scarred me for life. I'd get off my bike at the front door and grab eight folded newspapers from my basket. The glass doors of the nursing home were locked at night to keep the inmates in, so I'd put the newspapers under my arm and punch in the code. I'd take one more gulp of fresh air, as much as my 12-year-old lungs could hold, pull open the door, and step inside. The smell was so awful I could barely take it. I'd run down the corridor to the business administration office and drop the newspapers off. Even though I was holding my breath, I could *feel* the smell; stale urine, disinfectant, despair, decay, and old age. I'd turn and sprint back to the front door.

The worst part of my job was collecting the money. This was before the advent of automated billing and I was required to go door to door at the end of each month to collect the fare. When I went to the nursing home to collect the money, I'd have to wait for the manager to give me a check, once again assaulted by the smell. I'd sit there in the lobby, inhaling with reluctance, while the manager took her time with a pair of 50-year-olds who were there to get the sales pitch on behalf of their aging parent.

One day I was told to wait in an adjoining guest room, where the current short-term incumbent was on a "serenity walk" with a loving CNA. Inmates wearing hospital-style gowns and shower slippers shuffled past. It was like a march of the living dead to me—elderly people who had been cast off to the ghastly places that Dickens might have written about.

I sat alone on the guest's bed with my toes barely reaching the floor. After a moment, I felt my butt getting damp. I stood and felt the back pockets of my new jeans. They were wet. I turned and looked at the spot on the bed where I'd been sitting. It was wet too. I smelled my hands and recoiled from the stench of urine.

Nope, there was no way I was going to grow old. I committed myself to that.

———

Not all my jobs paid money. We were frequently roped into service projects through the church. Making unpaid matters worse, these service projects were almost always on a Saturday, which was the only day of the week I didn't have to go to school or church. I felt like Joan of Arc.

The Mormon church is one of the largest landholders in the country with significant holdings in Brazil and other foreign countries, too. It owns vast farms, including what they called stake farms. Those farms were managed by each individual stake (collection of wards) in the church. And who provided a lot of the labor to maintain the farms? You guessed it.

I was confused when we learned at church one Sunday that we were all being recruited to show up at the bishop's house at six a.m. on Saturday morning to go work at the stake farm. Why, I wondered, did everyone need to go work at my dad's office? No, Warren, you idiot. The stake farm, not State Farm. This was a disappointment because my dad actually paid me to work at his office and he always took us to the Hawaiian Restaurant across the street for lunch which had authentic indoor rainstorms and erupting volcanoes. It had been the only restaurant I'd been to that offered more than one utensil.

What fun we had at the stake farm pulling weeds and painting the stupid barn! Other times we had a ball down at the church's cannery, sweating over peaches and oily conveyor belts at seven o'clock on a Saturday morning when we could have been sleeping in. I can't say I even thought about the point of what we were doing, which was to replenish the food pantries so poor people could eat. Perhaps I should have boned up on the spirit and had a better attitude about slaving away like I did for a good cause.

16

ALMOST EVERYTHING IN MY YOUNG LIFE REVOLVED around the church and the ward. It was the central gathering spot for just about all we did. Usually it would be for a church service, but that wasn't all. Not by a long shot. For example, we held the ward bazaar inside the gymnasium. There were tables laden with homemade bread, jam, and canned fruits where the Sisters milled about sniffing and saying things like, "Oh, Sister Tidwell, why, that is the prettiest chocolate cake I have ever seen!" Whether it tilted and sagged a bit was beside the point. Of course, Sister Tidwell would then be compelled to make a generous comment about Sister Rasmussen's quilt.

The parking lot had been transformed into a carnival with a cotton candy machine and mechanical rides that wouldn't have passed a safety check by today's standards. There was a merry-go-round and about five ponies that walked around in a circle, tethered to a maypole. There was also one of those dunking machines where you sat above a five-foot-deep tub of cold water and people threw balls at a button. If they hit it, the seat gave way and you fell into the water. Guess who was the first one to get dunked? In fact, guess who was the *only* dad to get dunked? The other dads were too buttoned up, or too worried about getting wet, but my dad didn't care. This was *fun!*

After it was dark, we all filed into the gymnasium for the raffle. I won a paper airplane which was a relief because the other prize was a knitted doily. Then they turned off the lights and we watched *The Unsinkable Molly Brown* which was projected onto a large bed sheet hanging on the cinderblock wall. Children fell asleep in their parent's arms. It was as good as Christmas Eve.

The ward house was also the spot where we met for scouting. There was a strong link between our young Mormon men's groups and scouting. All Mormon boys were Boy Scouts. I'm pretty sure the Mormon church was the Boy Scouts' largest sponsor.

There was a boy in my scout troop, however, who wasn't Mormon. His name was Jeff. This was a curious thing. Jeff's not a Mormon? *Wah?* Who is this guy? He lasted about a month and then we never saw him again. Maybe he was turned off by scout meetings that started with a Mormon prayer and ended with the bishop telling us of our priesthood assignments or our Duty to God awards that required, among other things, that we pay a full tithing. This seemed perfectly sensible to me, but maybe his parents thought memorizing a passage from The Book of Mormon didn't seem pertinent to a First Aid merit badge.

My career as a Boy Scout actually began early, when I was about 5. My dad was the scoutmaster and hauled Danny and me around to all the events and camp outs (that's why we were premature entrants in the race to start a fire with flint and steel wool). My first memory as a quasi-scout was hiking up to Ensign Peak in Salt Lake City. It took ages and was utterly exhausting (I did it the other day in about 10 minutes). What I most remember about that hike was a boy in my dad's troop who had diabetes and had to have an insulin injection every day. This was about the most horrible thing I could possibly imagine. A shot every day? I would've rather died from diabetes, whatever that was. This boy was a loner, an outcast, and he had a face full of pimples. I remember the way my dad treated him like he was the coolest boy in the world—the way he had his arm around his shoulder and genuinely gave a shit about him.

I didn't learn much about scouting from scouting. Oh sure, I learned how to build a fire and turn on a Coleman stove. And I went through the motions so I could earn a few merit badges, the same way I'd approached school, doing just enough to be herded along with the rest of my troop. For example, I'd cram at the last minute to get my Geography merit badge, and then completely forget where Germany was.

What I *did* learn was much more valuable to me than Dutch oven cooking skills or the proper use of lighter fluid. I learned how to be cold, how to swear, how to chuck rocks, how to hike, and how to throw a pocket knife so it'd stick into a tree trunk. I learned about camaraderie with my buddies, most of whom were incorrigible hoodlums. (Oh, the fun we had spying on other campers, sneaking in to steal their food, collapsing their tents, or tying their duffel bags up in a tree. We'd be hiding in the forest nearby, laughing our heads off as we watched them return to their camps.) I learned how to tell scary stories around the camp fire at night, so scary in fact that we couldn't sleep because of Hyrum, the one-armed axe murderer who roamed the woods looking for kids to bludgeon.

My scout troop was basically the boys from my Sunday School class, a homogenous group of quasi-normal boys who were all indoctrinated into a belief in the golden tablets. I vividly remember lying in my sleeping bag under the stars after a day of tying knots and looking into the night sky. I remember seeing all those stars and wondering which one was Kolob, the specific orb where God lived. There were so many! Kolob was as real to me as the crackling embers of the fire as it wound down for the night.

Probably the most morally corrupt thing we did, far worse than stealing Snicker bars from neighboring camp sites, was the time we smoked rope. That's rope, not dope. We cut six-inch strands of nylon rope, lit one end, and smoked like we were Humphrey Bogart. It was so edgy, so *scandalous*. Smoking! Our scoutmaster made us stop because even though no smoke entered our lungs, we were supposed to avoid even the appearance of evil. And it also made no sense to start a forest fire.

The highlight every year was the Six-Day Camp. It was a camping trip up in the Uinta Mountains. There was a Boy Scout requirement that all scouts undergo a physical exam before going on such an extremely long and treacherous campout (where our tents were pitched a few yards from the station wagons). So, a week before the campout we'd all traipse over to Brother Vern Webb's house because he was a doctor. He listened to our heartbeats and shoved a popsicle stick down our throats to make us gag and say ahhh. Then we'd line up and pull down our pants while Brother Webb stuck his finger on our balls, then make us turn our heads and cough. It was a bit weird, all this ball touching, but I assumed that was the medically established way it was to be done (and it probably was). However, as I write this now, it sounds like Brother Webb should have been in jail, or at least on some sort of watch list.

One year I had the mumps and had to miss the first two days of camp. Since Bishop Reeves was going to drive up to the scout camp after work on Day Two, my mom arranged for me to hitch a ride with him. Oh, this was awkward, spending two hours alone in the car with our bishop. What on earth would we talk about? Would he want to quiz me about the scriptures, or perhaps the perils of masturbation? Would he demand to know which one of us 12-year-old miscreants was responsible for drawing the life-sized penis on the inside of the bathroom stall's door? And if so, would I hem and haw before finally ratting out Howard?

He picked me up in his roomy, burgundy Impala which drove like a boat and could have carried his Two-Year-Supply of food in the trunk. It was the nicest car I'd ever been in. It even had power windows. Obviously, Bishop Reeves was rich, which made it even more intimidating. I picture him now, heavy set, ruddy complexion, capillaries spreading across his cheeks, a light sheen of sweat in the afternoon summer heat, the few remaining strands of grayish hair desperately combed from one side of his shiny pate to the other. He didn't talk much to me, which was good. Instead he listened to a Nat King Cole tape, humming along with it. I must say he was very nice. I wondered if he felt sorry for me, coming as I did from such a large passel of kids and I imagined him muttering to himself, "Here's another one of Leonard and Helen's children, bless his little heart." On the other hand, I knew he respected my parents and made me feel like I was a cool kid.

That night, he gathered us all around the campfire for an impromptu testimony meeting. That's where everyone goes around in a circle and proclaims their devotion to the gospel and their certainty that Joseph Smith was indeed the prophet. That this occurred at a Boy Scout camp was not unusual. Indeed, it would have been unusual, unseemly even, if it hadn't occurred. It wasn't mandatory, this testimony giving, but it would have been really awkward when it came around to you and you deferred. What, cat's got your tongue? I parroted what all the other kids said, about how it was all so obviously true and how I knew beyond a shadow of a doubt that Joseph Smith was a true prophet. Then, after the fire burned low, someone would start off with a scary story about Hyrum.

Once every two months we'd have a Court of Honor where our scouting merit badges were awarded. We met in the cultural hall at the ward. The cultural hall was really the gymnasium and a lot went on in the gym. Everything from ward basketball to the ward banquets were hosted there. There was even the occasional wedding reception where the basketball hoops would be festively adorned with streams of crepe paper and the wedding party would be wedged between a table with a record player on one side and a table with punch and cookies on the other.

Picture about ten scouts, dressed to the nines in our uniforms, the sashes around our necks festooned with pins and merit badges like we were small General Pattons. Now picture me as my name is called to come forward to be honored with my Cooking merit badge. The scoutmaster, or perhaps the bishop, shaking my hand as I stand smiling, my blond hair sharply parted with an untamed cowlick. Picture my uniform, un-ironed, and my brown scout pants hanging two inches above my ankles. Someone in the audience is standing with a Polaroid Instamatic. I felt special, because I had never been singled out for anything.

On another overnight scouting adventure, we had to drive about two hours to get to the camp. There must have been four carloads of scouts and adult leaders. My dad was one of the volunteer dads. I was packed into another car and my dad drove a separate group in the final car of our caravan. At some point we passed a stranded car off the side of the road with its hood up.

Thirty minutes later, the first three cars rolled into camp and we spent the next half hour unpacking our stuff and setting up our tents. I could tell the other men were slightly annoyed at my dad. "Where's Leonard? I thought he was right behind us. He has the hamburger buns."

I didn't say anything, even though I knew exactly where my dad was. I knew it without a shadow of a doubt. I knew it without a prompt or a crystal ball.

Finally, I saw our family station wagon rumbling up the road. It pulled into our camp in a trail of dust and my dad got out, a smile on his face. His hands were covered in grease and oil and the back of his clothes were dirty from lying under the stranded car at the side of the road to help fix it.

That was my dad.

17

ONCE A MONTH, I'D GET PAIRED WITH an adult male in our ward to go Home Teaching. That was a church program where we'd visit a handful of families with a spiritual message. Usually the ward members we were visiting invited us in, and other times they pretended they weren't home. It's not like they resented us for coming, it was more that they were also doing the same thing to yet others in the ward. In other words, everyone was essentially "home teaching" everyone else.

I had no idea why they had to drag me along. I mean, it wasn't like I was going to bowl them over with a dissertation on the atonement. I wasn't Billy Graham. I'd just sit there like a bump on the log in the family's living room while the adults talked about the weather and gossiped about who the new bishop was going to be (it rotated among male members of the congregation about every five years and was a big prize for neighborhood prestige).

One time I tagged along with Brother Crofts to the Holmgren's house. Apparently, Brother Holmgren was a member of the John Birch Society. I thought he was a tree specialist, or someone like Johnny Appleseed, like he was an expert on birches or something.

Anyway, I surmised fairly quickly that Brother Crofts didn't like the John Birch Society because he and Brother Holmgren got into a big fight about it when we were supposed to be home teaching them about something with a spiritual angle. I didn't know what to do because I'd never seen adults shout at each other like that. Finally, Sister Holmgren told her husband that he was out of line and should apologize to us. "Honestly, Larry, you're acting like a child." I'll bet she and Brother Holmgren got into a fight after we left because, in all fairness, it'd been Brother Crofts who'd started the whole thing. As we drove away, Brother Crofts told me that Brother Holmgren was a complete idiot. I agreed with him because I didn't know what else to say.

One day when I was 12, my dad's junior home teaching companion bailed on him so my dad dragged me along even though I thought it was unfair that I would have to go twice in the same month. We'd been assigned to go to Brother and Sister Webb's house (the doctor in our ward who'd touched my balls and made me cough). I had a pretty bad stomach ache that evening and it kept getting worse. I wasn't too worried about it, but we were at Dr. Webb's house so I happened to mention it when he saw me sort of balled up on his sofa. He asked me to stand and then he poked my abdomen with his finger and asked me if it hurt. Well, yeah, it hurt, a little. I didn't know if he wanted me to tell him it hurt, or not. And, to be honest, it didn't hurt *that* much.

You've got an appendicitis, he declared. This sounded ominous. He told my dad I needed an appendectomy and I better hurry and get it before my appendix ruptured. That freaked me out because he said if it ruptured I could die. I could *die?* I could feel my internal appendix-clock ticking and I figured it was bound to rupture at any moment. And then what? I'd be dead, that's what. Right there on Brother and Sister Webb's oriental rug, lying in a pool of blood next to their glass coffee table. They'd all be staring down at me, ruminating on the calamity. "Geez, Leonard, I guess you shoulda brought him in sooner."

My grasp of anatomy was modest—I barely knew the hip bone was connected to the thigh bone—but this appendicitis diagnosis seemed rather hasty. There was something about the whole thing that just seemed a bit fishy, the notion that one little finger poke would be enough to declare me fit for an organ removal. I wanted to ask him if he was sure, if maybe we ought to invest in a second opinion or something. At a minimum, I wanted him to press on the spot again, maybe feel around a little bit more, maybe even touch my balls again. I mean, we were talking about one of my organs (well, almost an organ).

Doctor Webb told my dad to take me to the hospital and he'd be right behind us in his fancy Cadillac. He said he'd cut that grimy appendix out before it ruptured and spewed rotten appendix juice all over the place. My dad took me home first so he could tell my mom where we were going. Or, maybe it was to allow me to say my final goodbyes, I didn't know. My siblings were duly impressed. I was going to the hospital to have an operation, something they'd never done.

The next thing I knew, I was gowned and out like a light. I woke in my hospital room, appendix-less. Doctor Webb came to my hospital room the next day when my mom was there. He was wearing his white butcher coat and made quite a show about how lucky we were to have caught it in time, that when he saw my appendix with his own two eyes, why, it looked like it'd been ready to erupt all over the rest of my innards. I was very skeptical about this and even as a young boy I sensed an economic emergency on his part, like he was late on his boat payment or something.

That said, this operation was one of the coolest things that had ever happened to me. I felt special. I had the complete attention of my mom and my dad. Not only that, but I had my own room *with a TV!* They served me food in bed on a tray and I had root beer with one of those straws with the little accordion bends in it. It felt like I was the pharaoh or something.

Mormons believe in modern medicine, by the way. They aren't like those religious sects that shun doctors and pills. Actually, they believe in a combo approach—good modern medicine combined with the power of prayer. The tricky thing for me to understand was how to process it when the prayers didn't work. I'd been taught that the power of faith (which alone could move mountains) was further enhanced by the robust power of a priesthood blessing. I assumed if you packaged those two together with a one-two punch you could cure any illness. But I saw for myself it didn't work that way. I asked my parents about it and they said it all depended on faith. Some people just got better and some didn't. But what about the whole moving-mountain thing, I wondered? Geez, some wicked people with zero faith recovered without a single prayer said on their behalf. I knew God worked in mysterious ways, but it seemed rather hit and miss to me.

I recall overhearing some adult ward members talking about Christian Scientists who, apparently, didn't believe in going to the doctor. "Bunch of religious fanatics," they said. I tended to agree. On the other hand, I could see how it showed a lack of faith to go to the doctor. After all, if we *really* believed in God's power, then why would it be weird to just rely on that?

My parents weren't pill poppers. I took my first aspirin after I was married. My wife thought I was joking when I said I'd never taken one. "What if you had a headache?" she asked. But I don't get headaches. "Okay, what if you stubbed your toe really bad?" I don't stub my toes. "What if you have a cold? Don't you take cold medicine?" Do they have such a thing, I asked?

As a Mormon I believed in science, but only to the extent it didn't conflict with my religious beliefs. For example, it was troubling to hear the earth was billions of years old. It *was?* How could that be, I wondered? I thought the Bible said it was only 6,000 years old, give or take, so that must've been the real number. And you didn't even need to get me started on the theory of evolution.

The way I heard it, the claims of evolution were an insult to God. We didn't evolve, God made us in his own image. He made Adam first, then plopped him down into the Garden of Eden. Everyone with a brain in their head should've known that. And because Adam was lonely and needed to get the world's population going, God took one of his ribs and used it to make Eve. That sounded realistic enough to me. Now, I'll admit the bit about the talking serpent gave me some pause, as did God spazzing out over Eve eating the apple. It just seemed like an unnecessary overreaction. But these stories were nowhere near as far-fetched as evolution, which was such a whacky idea it just had to be made up by people who didn't believe in God.

———

We were teenagers and Danny had a painting job when he had a bad accident. One day he was on an extension ladder painting a third-story window. The feet of the ladder rested on the top of a two-story, flat-roofed building and spanned across a 10-foot alleyway to the window of another taller building where he was painting the window. Suddenly, the feet of the ladder slipped on the gravel roof and Danny fell into the alley three stories below, following the ladder the whole way down.

He was rushed to the hospital where his condition was touch and go. I was playing catch with Steve in our front yard when the neighbor ran across the street to tell my mom to get off the phone (she was probably gabbing with one of my aunts). My mom was frantic. Another neighbor came outside to see what the fuss was all about. Danny fell three stories and might die! This other neighbor, a raging Gentile if ever there was one, assured my mom that Danny would be okay. Kids were tough. And, besides, she said, "easy come, easy go."

I know how much that wounded my mom, how infuriating and crippling it was for this insensitive neighbor to have said such a thing. Easy come, easy go. So many Driggs children that if one of them died my parents could just pop out another one. I don't think my mom ever forgave her.

Danny survived, flourished actually, as a direct result of surgery. He had a blessing too, of course, and it's entirely possible it was the blessing that did the trick, that put him over the top. But I'd bet if my parents had been given the option to turn him over to the doctors for the surgery, or to the bishop for a blessing, they would have picked the doctor. And that's a curious thing when you think about it, because they always swore that faith could move mountains, and they had tons of faith. Then again, when the chips were *really* down, maybe they didn't have as much faith as they thought. Or maybe they were just padding the odds.

18

I WAS SITTING ON A FOLDING LAWN CHAIR with an aluminum frame and crisscrossed strips of nylon. I was wearing a tee shirt with wide horizontal stripes, just like one I'd seen on the cover of a Beach Boys album (another purchase from my newspaper route). It was a hot summer afternoon and there was an entire bowl of red cherries on my lap. I was eating them, one by one, and spitting the pits onto the grass. I was alone and it was one of the few contemplative moments of my young life.

Bishop Reeves had just died from a heart attack.

I sat there, spitting the pits, thinking about how awful it must have been for his children. Their dad died? It was hard to imagine such a thing. At his funeral they said such nice things about him, which were presumably true. (On the other hand, I had to wonder about these generous compliments because the only other funeral I'd been to at the time was my great grandmother's and they said she was the sweetest thing who'd ever lived. Ever? Sweet? All I remembered about her was that she was crotchety, and smelled funny.)

The funeral speakers said that God had called Bishop Reeves home, that there was a special need for him in heaven—a bigger assignment. God needed him in heaven? But why? Didn't heaven already have enough good ones? This suggestion that he'd been reassigned to heaven seemed illogical to me at the time, as if there was a more important place for him to be than with his wife and children. What was the rush? Couldn't God have waited a few more years? Couldn't he have waited at least until Doug was in junior high, or maybe until Debbie got her braces off? Far be it for me to question such a thing, because I wasn't a God yet, but I wouldn't have called him home so soon.

Bishop Reeves was a doctor to boot. Now, I knew doctors were not infallible, and they eventually died too, but I'll admit this threw me for an additional loop. He was young and had all the knowledge that doctors had and still he couldn't keep himself from dying. For some reason this scared me. We really *were* at God's mercy.

I remember leaning my head back and looking up to the sky. I didn't expect to see Kolob where God lived because we didn't know exactly which orb was his. And, besides, it was light outside. But still I peered and wondered. What would it be like to die? Does it hurt? Is an angel waiting there to escort you, or do you have to find your own way to heaven as a final test, like an eternal scavenger hunt? Obviously, I didn't want to die. I didn't want to be like my friend Rick Clissold.

I knew that when I died, I'd run into my grandparents who were already dead. I figured I'd recognize them, but then again, I wondered. Would they be the same age they were when they died? Like, would my Grandpa Driggs be a 40-year-old strawberry farmer and my Grandpa West be a bald, wrinkled 93-year old? That didn't seem fair. And would Rick Clissold have both his legs or just the one? Then I remembered that we believed we'd be resurrected to our perfect age. But what in the heck was my perfect age? What if my perfect age was 80 and my mom's perfect age was 20? Would I be four-times as old as my own mom?

I pondered and spit until the bowl was empty and then got sick from all the cherries, so sick in fact that I wanted to die.

———————

I decided to run for President of the seventh grade. I figured as long as I was throwing my hat into the ring and had to make all those posters and give a skit in the auditorium in front of the entire student body, I might as well go for President instead of Vice. I mean, who runs for Vice President? Or Secretary? It makes no sense.

My mom was the creative genius of the campaign (I doubt my dad even knew I was running, and if he did, he would've said that I'd win in a landslide, easily). We took my younger brother Matt's toilet seat, the kind you use for potty training, and glued it to a poster which I hung in the main hallway of the junior high school. My slogan was *Seat Driggs in Office*. (I didn't get it at first—I was only 12.)

All the talks I had to give in church had helped prepare me for the bright lights, but still I was scared shitless when I walked on stage to face the electorate. I said something about how I'd be such a good seventh grade president, without knowing what a seventh-grade president even did, and then waited for the primary vote. I made the top two which meant I had to give a skit the following week. Danny and I dressed up like doctors and operated on our buddy, Roger Olson, who laid on a gurney and we pulled spaghetti out of his gut like it was his real intestines. I don't recall the point of this surgical reenactment and why it would've made me a better seventh grade president than Rob Neff.

I've never been so nervous in my whole life during the school assembly the next day when they announced the winners. They first announced the Secretary and Vice-Presidential winners, booby prizes to be sure, and then came the big moment. I pretended I didn't care, and so did Rob. The place was going bananas when they called my name. My reaction was immediate relief. And then I felt bad for Rob. I was very happy I'd won, but I knew how stupid he must have felt, clapping as if he was *glad* I'd won. I would have done the same thing, clapped away, inches from bawling, pretending to everyone in the auditorium that I'd forgotten I'd even been on the ballot.

I was wearing my favorite horizontally striped tee shirt and Sea Fare jeans because I knew everyone would be looking at me. And they did look as I shrugged my shoulders, pretending to be so humble. Oh, yeah, that's right, I almost forgot. I was running, wasn't I? Ha!

I wonder if my best friends even voted for me. Of course, they *said* they did—they said they'd never been happier in their entire lives with my big win. But it is quite possible they voted for Rob because they didn't want me soaring to unprecedented heights of popularity, leaving them behind with the losers who played the trombone in the school band and wore headgear. On the other hand, Rob's best friends probably didn't vote for him either, so it may have come out in the wash.

I don't think my stardom changed me. In fact, everything stayed pretty much the same. I still couldn't make the volleyball team.

My tenure was marked with mediocrity. There was only one time when my political skills were required. I was supposed to lead the student body in the Pledge of Allegiance that fall during an assembly on health and hygiene, but I was sick that day. So, all in all, my political career was a dud.

————

It was shortly after the junior high Election of 1967 that we remodeled the basement. Danny and I had been sharing a room the size of a walk-in closet when my dad thought it would be nice if we had our own rooms. Amen to that! The plan was to erect a wall down the center of the room. This created two rooms, each smaller than the average nun gets in an old convent after taking her chastity vows.

We drove down to the lumberyard to buy the two-by-fours and the sheets of faux-wood paneling. I picked a light blond paneling color and Danny picked a mahogany. We folded the station wagon's seats down (we were always folding them down for *something*) and then sat on the sheets of paneling with the hatchback open so they wouldn't slide out on the ride home. This project was exciting.

When finally finished, my room smelled like sawdust and was so cozy it barely fit my twin bed. But it was mine. I taped Sports Illustrated photos of baseball players from floor to ceiling. (This was well before SI produced their annual swimsuit issue, which would have made for marvelous wall décor. In the meantime, I put up pictures of Pete Rose and Willie Mays because I was a baseball nut, reading the box scores in the newspaper before delivering it every morning.)

Danny's room was only the width of a two-by-four away from mine (without insulation) and he had a Magnavox turntable which played music all the time. It was the druggy kind of music, too—the rock and roll that was so perilously close to sin, flirting with the sticky corners of wickedness. Spirit. Cream. Neil Young. Buffalo Springfield. Crosby Stills and Nash. The Doors. The Beatles. The Beach Boys. But the worst album he had (by worst I mean the one that may have crossed the line) was Black Sabbath. Even the name of the band made me queasy. *Black Sabbath?* Do you *want* to go to hell, Danny?

I'd lie in bed and listen to his stack of records play. When a record was finished there'd be the scratchy sound for a moment and then I'd hear the next one drop. Another scratchy sound and then the needle would catch the groove. Don't get me wrong, I liked rock and roll, I just didn't want to tease the demarcation line of sin—the DMZ between heaven and hell.

I don't recall my parents making too much of a fuss about the long hair, bangs, beards, and St. Pepper stuff. I think they were so busy changing diapers and keeping us fed that they frankly didn't care if daddy took the T-bird away, or not. But other parents were flipping out. The country was going to hell in a handbasket. All these drugs. And this nonsense over Peace. What was it with these peaceniks anyway? I know a lot of my friend's parents who had older kids were about at the end of their ropes with all this lovey-dovey peace crap. They wanted to wipe out the Viet Cong once and for all, because if we bombed the godless bastards to smithereens, we'd show them that democracy was the only way to ensure peace. "But," I heard Brother Garner explain, "they aren't even Christians, so they don't value life like we do."

I had long hair when I was a teenager. Real long hair. It wasn't a sign of rebellion, or a statement that I didn't believe in the golden tablets. It was just cool to have long hair, that's all. My dad didn't care about that kind of stuff. He wasn't the crewcut, military-style disciplinarian type. I don't think he cared about my hippie clothes either. He wouldn't have noticed or cared whether a man wore an orange prison jumpsuit or an expensive Italian blue-pinstripe. He was neither impressed nor unimpressed with what someone wore, or drove, or what kind of house they lived in. He wore whatever my mom bought him (and it didn't look like she wanted to turn him into a clothes horse).

But my mom cared what I wore. At least once. I thought she was going to have a coronary when I bought a tee shirt with the picture of a guy riding a Kawasaki motorcycle on the front (I had a Kawasaki dirt bike at the time and terrorized the neighborhood with it). The caption beneath the picture read: "Put something exciting between your legs." I didn't even think my mom would get it because she was nearly 40-years-old at the time. But she got it, all right. I eavesdropped on my parent's conversation that night. My dad was trying to talk her off the ledge.

"Listen, Helen, I don't think we should overreact—it's not that big of a deal," he said.

"Not that big of a deal? Listen to yourself! Have you even read it?" I think my mom worried I was headed straight for the sexual deviant watchlist.

"Warren's a good kid," he said. "I think we need to trust his judgment."

"Trust his *judgment?* So, what, you think this is *okay?* You think it's okay for our son to waltz around advertising sexual intercourse on his tee shirt? You mark my words, Leonard. This is how it starts."

It was resolved I wouldn't wear it, at least when my mom was around.

19

ONE SUNDAY EACH MONTH WAS DESIGNATED AS Fast Sunday. I hated Fast Sunday. All kids hated Fast Sunday and the adults probably did too, they just pretended they didn't. Fast Sunday actually began Saturday evening, and then no food or drink for 24 straight hours. My parents, as devout as they were, had a slightly relaxed view of the timing, so we didn't have to start fasting at our house until Sunday morning. I once set my alarm for 11:45 and had a bowl of cereal to top off my stomach before going back to bed. I figured my parents delayed the start of the family fast until Sunday morning because they didn't want to do battle with us trying to sneak a scoop of porridge. Or maybe they were just hungry too.

The way I understood it, fasting was supposed to bring us closer to God. How, I didn't know. If this was its purpose, I can only say it backfired. I didn't like God for it. We didn't eat all that much to begin with and I was usually starving, and now this? How was I supposed to harness the Christian spirit and really delve into the principles of the atonement when all I could think of was food? The simple answer was, I couldn't. The other purpose of the fast was to help those in need. We'd take the money we would have spent on food and donate it to the church so they could dole it out to poor people. This seemed like a good idea, but I didn't understand why we couldn't just donate the money to poor people so they could eat and us eat, too. I didn't get why it had to be mutually exclusive. Couldn't we all just eat?

After Sunday School, the young men in our ward (that would be Eric, Steve, Howard, me, and about 20 of my other baby-boomer buddies) would walk through the neighborhood, door to door, to collect the fast offerings. We had a stack of small envelopes with a family's name printed on each one. They were the kind of envelope with the little string that wraps around and around the flap to close it.

Ding dong. "Hi, I'm here to collect your fast offerings." Okay, they'd say, let me go get my checkbook. I'd wait on the porch and they'd bring back the envelope, the string wrapped snugly so I wouldn't open it to see if they were tightwads who didn't care about hungry poor people. Or maybe they worried I might steal the money inside, which never occurred to me. Why would I be dumb enough to steal something that belonged to God? He'd see me because he saw everything. Besides, what was I supposed to do with a five-dollar check made payable to the Valley View Fifth Ward? I knew it was none of my business how much they'd donated, but still I wondered. Especially with the rich people in the ward, the ones who drove Cadillac Sevilles, wore mink stoles, and hired other people to mow their lawns.

There was one man on my route who lived in an iron lung. He spent his life in a casket-looking thing parked in his living room so he could breathe. I still had to ask him for money.

But I'll tell you the worst thing was going to the house of a Jack Mormon (or, as I mentioned before, sometimes referred to as an Inactive). Jack Mormons were still on the records of the church but had shed the light of truth like a fur coat on a hot summer day. They were the ones who drank coffee and didn't go to church very often, or, god forbid, not at all. Take the Hobson's for example. I'd go to their house, knowing full well they'd probably only put a dollar in the envelope, if that, and grudgingly do it because they didn't believe in the gold tablets. Or at least they didn't act like it.

I'd like to report that I felt sorry for these Jack Mormons—felt sorry for them because they must have known they were headed straight for the Terrestrial Kingdom. And if they weren't careful, they might even drop all the way down to the Telestial. But the truth is I was jealous of them, at least on Fast Sunday. I'd ring their doorbell and immediately be assaulted by the smell of bacon wafting from their house. I swear I could smell it seeping right through the mortar of their bricks. The door would open and they'd be holding a cup of coffee. They weren't dressed in their church clothes, but rather in comfy casuals, enjoying their day off. They seemed happy. (I knew this happiness was an act, because how could you be genuinely happy living in a state of unbridled sin? Not even going to *church?*) They'd invite me in while they rummaged around for five dollars. The smells were torture. Bacon, eggs, toast. I was *starving* and there they were, living high on the hog, practically rubbing my nose in it. I could only hope I'd get the last laugh after I died when I vaulted past them straight up to the Celestial Kingdom. Hope that bacon was worth it!

Of course, then there were the Rigtrup's. They were church-goers but watched television on Sunday, a marginal no-no (unless it was a faith-inspiring program, like The Spoken Word). Brother Rigtrup invited me to take a load off and sit for a few minutes to watch the football game. What was I supposed to do? I didn't want to be *rude*. And the San Francisco 49'ers were my favorite team. So, there I sat, on Fast Sunday, watching the 49'ers beat the Bears as Sister Rigtrup strolled past with a mug of coffee, dragging the smell of pancakes with her. I didn't know if I'd be eternally punished for watching the game, or if I'd be handsomely rewarded for turning down a pancake.

Once we'd gathered all the money, we'd return to the church for Fast and Testimony Meeting. That's where members of the congregation were encouraged to stand and tell the rest of the crowd how much they believed, and why they believed it. As a deacon (that's what they called us 12-year-olds) my job was to keep my eyes peeled on the congregation and when one of them stood, I was to deliver the portable microphone to them. If they were middle-pew, I'd hand it to the guy on the aisle and then it'd be passed down the row, cable trailing. Ward members also had the option of walking up to the pulpit to give their testimonies.

It was always awkward when no one stood. You could hear the sound of silence exponentially build as church members furtively looked around to see who'd stand up next. There was a direct relationship between the length of the Silence Gap and the sudden, urgent need for women to look through their purses, or the men to suddenly find some reason to study their hymn books as if they couldn't possibly stand *now*. But, alas, there were always The Regulars who'd bail everyone else out. These were Saints who basically liked to hear themselves talk. They'd stand and give a travelogue of their trip to Yellowstone, or report that their brother-in-law had been canned from his job, prayed, and got a new one in Denver. Sometimes they'd give a wholesale endorsement of how Jesus had changed their lives, but other times it might only be a little ditty about getting new shag carpet in the rumpus room. Rarely was I moved.

Then there were the parents who elbowed their children to stand. I was one of those kids. Talk about terrifying, that moment you stood. The entire congregation immediately turned to stare. It was deathly quiet while you waited for Howard, or some other 12-year-old in an ill-fitting, hand-me-down sport coat to get the danged mic to you. When it finally came down the row, you gripped the mic and began to broadcast your knowledge of the truth. It was always the same speech because every kid, without exception, said the exact same thing: *I know the church is true. I know Joseph Smith was a Prophet of God. I know The Book of Mormon is true. I love my mom and dad. In the name of Jesus Christ, Amen.* Doesn't sound too difficult, right? Well, I'm here to tell you it was.

Everyone in the congregation would smile and tilt their head at the sheer faithfulness of the poor child and his rote testimony of the truth. I'd hand the mic off and sit down. My proud parents would lean over a bit so they could see me down the pew wiping my sweaty palms on my pants. "Ahhh, look, Leonard, it's Warren." They'd smile their approval, satisfied to know that I had such a profound testimony of the gospel. I was determined to believe, too, especially after going through such trials and tribulations as bearing my testimony. It made absolutely no sense to go through all that for nothing.

By far, the most memorable Fast and Testimony meeting occurred when I was about 12. I was sitting with my buddies on the front row, eyes peeled and a portable mic in my hand, when Brother Wyatt stood. He walked down the aisle, and up to the pulpit. Brother Wyatt was familiar to me, but only because he was married to Sister Joy Wyatt, who had once been my Cub Scout den mother. He started yammering on about something we didn't care about, something about Joseph Smith blah blah blah, when suddenly his voice rose a few octaves. I looked up at the bishopric (who all sat on the podium behind the pulpit) and saw they were starting to fidget. What was the meaning of this, I wondered? I looked behind me at the audience and people were elbowing each other. I turned back to the front and saw the bishop had now stood and was approaching Brother Wyatt. The bishop touched him on the sleeve and whispered something to him. It was obvious he was trying to get Brother Wyatt to shut up. So I listened closer to what he was saying.

It immediately became clear to me what the problem was. Brother Wyatt was testifying at full throttle that the church had abandoned the truth when it stopped practicing polygamy. Polygamy, he was practically shouting, had been divinely inspired by none other than Joseph Smith who'd said it was the only way to heaven. And Brother Wyatt, for one, had had enough of all this namby-pamby monogamy and was imploring the rest of us to open our danged eyes. He was frantically thumbing through his Mormon scriptures to find the exact page where it'd been unequivocally commanded.

The bishopric was now on full alert, trying to remove him from the pulpit, gently at first and then tugging at the sleeve of his sport coat as Brother Wyatt hung on with one hand to the pulpit. It took three of them to pry him away before he got in a few more zingers about the joys of polygamy. It was the most exciting thing that had ever happened in church.

Brother Wyatt was allowed to stick around for the remainder of the service and I turned around to stare at him along with everyone else as he took his seat next to Sister Wyatt, whose head was down. I guess we all knew then that her husband didn't think she was enough.

The silence gap was longer than ever after all that excitement. Finally, one of The Regulars stood and testified that the church was spot on, monogamy was the only way to go, and that Joseph Smith was a true prophet. Then he brought the rest of us up to speed on the progress of his basement remodel.

————————

The best part of Fast and Testimony Meeting was the sacrament. We had a sacrament of bread and water that was passed down the pews on silver trays. First there was the tray of bread, broken up into one-inch pieces of Wonderbread, which Jesus said in the Bible was supposed to remind us of his body. This concept seemed a bit odd and I could never wrap my head around it. I mean, was I supposed to be thinking about his body when I chewed? And then there was the water, also passed down the pews in a tray filled with thimble-sized paper cups of water. The water was supposed to symbolize Christ's blood, which I always found to be rather disturbing. It just felt wrong to be drinking Jesus's blood, even symbolically, like I was a vampire or something.

I knew many Christian churches went with wine instead of water because that is technically what the Bible said you were supposed to do, but we believed that would be a liquid sin. (My Sunday School teacher told me the Bible *meant* to say "grape juice" instead of "wine" but it had been mis-translated over the centuries, obviously by some uninformed sinner like King James who had never heard of the Word of Wisdom.)

The sacrament was the best part of the service because I'd be starving by then. Even a small piece of bread tasted like manna from heaven. So I'd try to sneak a few auxiliary pieces like the rest of my buddies.

After sacrament meeting, we'd go home to a rump roast.

The summer after my landslide election win, the entire family went on a road trip to Mexico. My parents rented a trailer (this just *had* to be my dad's idea) and hauled it behind the station wagon all the way to Mazatlán. I don't know what my parents had been thinking. Summer? Nevada? Arizona? Mexico? How we fit, how we managed, I haven't a clue. I was a kid and didn't really care that I had a small little corner of the trailer which felt like a sauna. Hey, it was fun going on a road trip! I bought a switch blade and played with that thing the whole time. I'd whip it out, push the button and, *shazam!* Switchblade! I thought I was Zorro and I desperately wanted to stab something.

It was the summer of 1968 and I was 12. We were in a Mexican restaurant in Mazatlán sharing rice and beans when my dad overheard the table of Gringos next to us talking about how Robert Kennedy had just been assassinated. Another Kennedy gunned down. This, I knew, was awful.

I was not a fighter. I've only been in one legitimate fistfight in my whole life. I won it, too. In fact, I'm prepared to say I won it handily and if Randy Chamberlain ever reads this and takes exception to it that's his business. Let him tell his posterity that he beat me if it'll make him feel better.

Randy thought he was so tough. He kept coming up behind me and flipping my ear. When I'd finally had enough, I challenged him to a fight. It didn't last long. He hit me once and it didn't even hurt because the adrenaline was pumping full steam. But Randy, poor Randy, got my best. I probably hit him five times in the face. I've never been more relieved when a bunch of other guys broke it up.

After the fight, I went home to my room, closed the door, and started bawling. It wasn't the physical pain (I had none, but I'll bet Randy did), it was just all the emotional relief of getting it over with, ending my lifetime record at 1-0.

The time I got beaten up was by an adult, so I don't think it should count against my record. Howard, Eric, and I were throwing snowballs at cars. One late evening we were hiding behind some bushes next to Eric's house when I let one fly. The driver slammed on his brakes and slid to a stop on the icy road. We took off. This guy was about 30-years-old and must've been a track star. After we'd run about three blocks, we thought we were in the clear and fell on the snow laughing our heads off. "Holy crap, Howard, he almost caught us!" Suddenly, there he was, 10 feet away, charging. I don't know why he chose me, but he did. He smacked me a couple times and washed my face with snow. I took it like a man, never said a word. When he left, I looked around for my friends but they had run.

I tracked them down in Howard's basement. Gol, Driggs, that dude was pissed! We thought he was gonna kill you! Uh huh, so that's why you scrammed, leaving me to die in the snow. Thanks a lot. I wasn't badly hurt but I embellished it a bit, even suggesting that I had gallantly fought back and given the guy a little of his own medicine.

That night we slept in Howard's basement. We conjured up the horrifying thought that the guy in the souped-up Camaro would come back to finish us off. I had a tough time sleeping anyway because Howard's dad was a big-game hunter who displayed the casualties of his testosterone in the basement where we slept. There were mounted heads of all shapes and sizes hanging on the walls, glassy eyed, staring at me like I'd been the guy who'd shot them. Buffalo, big-horned sheep, warthogs, cougars. It freaked me out. There was a chair covered with some kind of brownish pelt next to a glass-topped table with elephant tusks for legs. A zebra, sans head and hooves, was splayed out on the floor. The walls that were not adorned by heads of dead beasts, displayed photos of Howard's dad, standing next to his kill, smiling, holding the bazooka that he'd used.

Howard's dad was in the bishopric (that's basically next in line to become the bishop), so I figured he had God's blessing for this recreational killing. But still I wondered. It didn't seem very God-like to go around shooting animals for sport, cutting off their heads, and then hanging them on the living room wall next to a portrait of Jesus. I could've understood it if a hyena or rabid hedgehog had sneaked into their house after they'd left the back door open and Howard's dad had to defend the homestead. But these animals had been shot in the African wild, where I figured God had put them.

20

MARK BURTON HAD THE COOLEST TREE HUT I'd ever seen. It wasn't like the rickety contraption we built in Steve's backyard in the crotch of a maple using rusty nails that we had to straighten and reuse, and old pieces of lumber we found in the vacant lot next door. Mark's hut was first class all the way.

Mark's dad had all the tools—electric saws, levels, and every kind of nail you could think of. We used them all, too, because we knew our tree hut could always use a few more nails, somewhere. The hut was big, so big in fact that we thought about subdividing it like we'd done in our basement. Oh, we dreamed big! We even talked about putting electricity in. We'd have a television, lamps, and a clock radio. Mark even talked about installing an oven but I thought that was overkill because none of us cooked much.

We climbed up to our tree hut with hammers, saws, and mouths full of nails. All of us except for Bruce Woodruff, anyway. He wasn't climbing up the makeshift ladder we hammered into the trunk of the tree. He was hunkered down over his mom's sewing machine a block away, making curtains for the hut.

Mark wasn't crazy about letting Bruce help build the tree hut in the first place because he claimed Bruce had tried to "touch him on the dick" at a sleepover. But Mark's mom insisted Bruce be included because she was such good friends with Bruce's mom. I didn't know if Mark ever told his mom about the sleep-over incident, or if it was even true. For all I knew, Mark just had it out for Bruce because Bruce threw like a girl. He'd be the guy in right field, picking his nose, oblivious that the score was tied in the bottom of the sixth inning. "Be alive out there," the coach would yell. Bruce hardly even seemed to care that we were playing the Giants. I mean, come on, the Giants were our biggest rival! They were the ones with the psycho coach who'd gone ballistic. We all hoped no Giant batter would hit one out to right field and interrupt Bruce's hunt for a four-leaf clover.

We stared at Bruce in amazement when he told us that he was riding his bike home to sew some curtains for the hut and wondered what color we thought might look good. Curtains? Color? Was he from Mars? After he left, we all teased him behind his back. We thought he deserved it. We didn't even like the way he talked. For example, we all had to go swimming in a mountain lake at scout camp to earn a merit badge. The water was freezing. Bruce emerged from the water and said, "It's cold water, but great fun!" Huh? *Great fun?* Did he live in the 18th century? We thought we were better than Bruce and he deserved to be ridiculed.

I would have been grossed out if Bruce had tried to touch me on the dick, and I probably would have hit him. And yet, if Debbie Ludlow had done the exact same thing I would have been honored. In fact, I would have promptly asked her to Homecoming.

I was just lucky to be heterosexual because I was taught that homosexuality was as sinful as anything you could think of (armed robbery, coffee, treason). That a man be heterosexual was so fundamental to Mormonism, so crucial to his role as an embryonic God, that to embrace the notion of homosexuality was to turn your back on God's plan. Maybe that's why BYU had a revolutionary treatment for the effective elimination of gayness. Namely, Electro Shock Therapy.

The therapy consisted of putting an array of electrodes around the base of a gay man's penis, and then show him pictures of nude men. If he became aroused, he'd get shocked right smack dab on the Johnson. All the subjects were Mormon men who'd volunteered for the treatment because they'd been told they needed to change, or face the music in hell. As part of the therapy, the gay man could select his own shock levels ranging from mild to severe. Many men picked the highest level of pain, so determined were they for a cure.

They don't do this therapy anymore, only when I was a teenager. Now they try to cure homosexuality with prayer. The reason they no longer do the shock treatment is not because the church has changed its tune on gayness, but simply because it didn't work. The only thing the men had to show for their pain and humiliation was a bright red penis.

When I was in my 20s, a friend of mine came out. His name was Gary and he was a nice man, but it horrified his fellow ward members. One of them said to me, "I don't get it. Why don't we just buy Gary a Playboy? I bet that'd fix him."

I was taught that God didn't make gay people, so it stood to reason that Gary and my friend Bruce must not have been gay right out of the chute—it was something they chose later on in life, like when they were 11 or 12. My church leaders said that God wouldn't make a reject. This made sense to me. On the other hand, when I asked my parents about the boy down the street who we referred to simply as The Mongoloid, they said that was different—he was special to God, in a *good* way. Therefore, I concluded that physical defects like, say, Down syndrome, were good in God's eyes but if it was something you chose, like homosexuality, then it was bad. I don't remember having to make that kind of dreadful choice, which was good, because I didn't want to pack my bags for the Telestial Kingdom.

As for Bruce, he was determined to be one of the boys, so he toiled away in his mom's sewing room making us curtains for Mark's tree house.

21

HOWARD WAS A SEX FIEND. IT WAS all he wanted to talk about. He even wanted to talk about my parent's sexual habits and he didn't beat around the bush. "Gol, your parents have done it *eight times.*" Eight times was extreme, I knew, and that was before they did it again—twice—and had my brothers Steve and Andy. Meanwhile, Howard strutted around with a smug look on his face because his parents had only done it five times, which seemed like a more reasonable number. Indeed, I was horrified, absolutely *horrified*, to know my parents had done it that many times. I mean, were they sex addicts? Did they need some kind of treatment? Frankly, I was embarrassed for them.

I wasn't obsessed with the sex topic myself, having been duly satisfied with the Mormon Factory Speech. The gist of the Factory Speech was that boys were like little factories, producing the power to create life, and sometimes they needed to blow off a little steam through their chimney. This seemed sensible enough to me. I didn't need more.

But then my dad, seemingly out of nowhere, decided to throw me into full blown therapy when he sat me down to tell me the truth about how my little factory operates.

We were sitting on the plaid sofa in the living room and it was strangely quiet in the house. I didn't know where everyone else was, but I suppose my dad wanted to hurry through his fatherly duty while it was quiet and no one else was around. At the time, I presumed he wanted to talk to me about my dismal report card, which would have been odd because I'd never shown it to my parents and they'd never asked. That wasn't the topic, however.

I wasn't like most kids who assumed their parents didn't know anything about sex, being so old and all. No, I knew my parents were freaking experts on the subject, having done it eight times by then. So I figured my dad knew what he was talking about, even though I didn't want to hear him talk about it.

I knew it needed to be said—I knew I eventually needed to be told The Facts. But couldn't he have warmed up to the subject, maybe have been a tad vaguer? I mean, was it necessary to come right out of the gate talking about penises and vaginas? Dad, please stop, I get it—a boy has a penis and a girl has that other thing (I couldn't bear to say the word). Wouldn't it have been enough to leave it there? Was it really necessary to tell me the boy actually sticks it *in* the girl? Say *wah?* He'd been so needlessly *graphic*. I imagined my mom eavesdropping from the other room, mortified, the back of her hand to her forehead, practically passing out.

———

At some point afterwards, the topic of sex came to preoccupy my thoughts. My adolescent balls were so blue they were practically navy. Even Sister Lindquist, the 50-year-old church organist with child bearing hips, caused me to have a sexual thought. I could've even made a case for Wilma Flintstone. What in God's name was happening to me!

My job at Lagoon introduced a particularly grim situation. We had to wear uniforms with our shirts tucked in. I'd walk around with my little broom, dust pan, and a permanent boner. There was only one way to hide it, but I was reprimanded every time I was caught with the front tail of my shirt untucked. What was I supposed to say? What was my defense for this flagrant dress code violation? That I was trying to hide my boner? I tried thinking about dead dogs in the street, ginger snaps, baseball—anything at all. It was no use.

I saw my first pornographic photo at church. We were in the downstairs bathroom, three of us in a stall with Howard, who'd smuggled in a Playboy. Our eyes almost popped out of our heads. We were speechless. It was the most glorious thing we'd ever seen. Howard hid it in a pyracantha bush outside the ward house. We looked at it every day for a week, even after it got wet from the sprinklers which caused it to become swollen thick. I can still see Miss July sprawled out fetchingly on that bear-skin rug. She wanted to be a journalist and rescue stray animals and all I wanted to do was marry her.

To me, sex was like an itch on my back that I couldn't quite get to, right between the shoulder blades that neither hand could reach. I knew I hadn't designed my factory—God had—so I didn't know what to make of my obsession.

I spent many nights under the stars with the scouts. I had a compulsion to see images of human shapes in the stars. And when I say humans, I mean females. I would lie in my sleeping bag and gaze up at the twinkly sky. Ahh, there was a breast. Oh, and there was a pair of lusty thighs. I could find erotica in almost any constellation.

Leave it to Howard to ask our Sunday School teacher, Sister Baxter, about Adam and Eve having babies. She reminded us they had Cain and Abel. Okay, but then what, he asked? Where did it go from there? Sister Baxter didn't know—she wasn't in the Garden of Eden when all this was happening. Howard then help-fully reminded the class that after Adam and Eve died, somebody must've kept having babies and the only thing he could think of was that Cain and Abel must've done it with their sisters. These were the things Howard spent his time thinking about, because he was just as bad as I was, if not worse. Naturally, his questions made Sister Baxter unhappy and I'll bet she called his parents. I myself thought Howard had made a good point, creepy as it was, that our earliest ancestors must've been incestuous. I tried not to think about it too much.

We were taught that our bodies were temples and we needed to keep them clean and pure and not allow them to be defiled by Satan and his bag of dirty tricks. Satan was everywhere, lurking. Sometimes you'd see evidence of his mischief, like if a girl became pregnant. I mean, it'd be right out in the open, right? But more often than not, Satan just lurked, circling like a shark's fin. The fin might slip under the water, but you knew the shark was there, close by, waiting to devour you. You had to be constantly wary. I sometimes felt like I was jumping from one lily pad to another, horrified of missing one and splashing into the clutches of Lucifer's shark-like jaws, swallowed whole in one evil gulp.

Because our bodies were pure, and because sex before marriage was unholy, even filthy, we were constantly warned not to let our guard down. Sex could only lead to unhappiness, and that's why we were supposed to save it for the person we married.

My first kiss happened behind John Cushing's house. We were

playing Truth or Dare, all of us sitting on his back lawn on a late summer night. Her name was Patti and I would have proposed to her that night but I had only finished the seventh grade and didn't have a ring.

The girl I would *not* have married was Cami. She was a Gentile. I went out with her a few times in high school because she was the most attractive girl at school, but her lack of faith in the truth was a disqualifier. That's the way it was in my community. You didn't date outside the faith. I mean, you could, but why would you? It might lead to love, and then what? You couldn't get married (well, you could I supposed, but that would disappoint the Saints and Gentiles both). Anyway, Cami, probably because she was a Gentile, wanted to test the limits of my chastity. She basically wanted to go to third base with me when she hadn't even gone to first base with God, so disbelieving was she. But would I be beguiled? Absolutely not (to my later profound regret).

Getting on base at all was a sin. There was no public flogging, no rap on the knuckles with a ruler, or any other visible punishment (unless what you did was really bad, which I'll tell you about in a moment). Instead you suffered the feeling of disapproval, of having let them down. You suffered the knowledge that you were a Chosen One and dropped the ball. And because Mormons were God's handpicked Chosen People, you'd feel you let down the entire church if not the gospel itself.

Now, if what you'd done was *really* bad, you were called out. Publicly. Take Brother Alstead and Sister Rehnquist, for example. Obviously, they'd misbehaved, together, in dramatic fashion. I only know this because one sacrament meeting the bishop stood and announced with somber, heartfelt disappointment that Brother Alstead and Sister Rehnquist had been excommunicated from the church. You could've heard the tiniest gasp in the audience if you'd known what to listen for, and then the stunned silence. You mean Brother Alstead who was married to Shirleen Alstead? And Sister Rehnquist whose husband was in the freaking bishopric? I was old enough to connect the dots and desperately wanted to know the particulars. Like how many times they'd done it, and where. Regrettably, the bishop was scant with the details so everyone was left to speculate. And trust me, everyone did. I even pictured them doing it. After all, Sister Rehnquist was hot, though for the life of me I couldn't figure out what she saw in Brother Alstead—she could have done a lot better, even within the slim pickings of our ward boundaries.

I specifically wondered, given my own predilections, what it was like for the bishop to hear Sister Rehnquist's confession. I know I would've preferred hearing that confession from her than hear her complain about her gallstones, or that she was tired of teaching the 5-year-olds in Sunday School and wanted to be the ward chorister instead.

When Saints sinned (and they did, for despite the fact that they were the Chosen People, they weren't perfect) they had to go through the steps of repentance to wipe the slate clean. A crucial step in the process was the confession. That made us all big confessors. The guilt would build and build like a steam boiler until it was ready to blow, and when it did you'd be wise to be sitting in your bishop's office because that is where the bulk of the confessing was done.

Growing up, I was always a tad bitter about this, wishing I were Catholic instead when it came to confessing. The way I heard it, Catholics went into a dark confessional booth and whispered to the priest through the little window, describing what bad thing they'd done. I figured they could even have disguised their voice so the priest wouldn't know it was actually Larry O'Brien who'd gone to that titty bar in Vegas. And then they were instructed to do a few Hail Mary's and call it a day. That didn't sound nearly as bad as what *we* had to do.

We had to confess to the bishop in his office with the lights on, right out in the open, sitting across the desk from him while he looked you dead in the eye. The temptation was always to play it down, maybe leave out the zestiest parts. But if you did that, it wouldn't be a full confession and you'd only be hurting yourself. Besides, the bishop would still know you were a lying, cheating, horny, embezzling, gossipy, covetous, Sabbath-Day breaking, coffee-drinking sinner. And there'd still be that smudge, that demerit for not coming 100% clean. It was better to let it rip, get it all out. You were supposed to feel better when you did—when you confessed your sins completely and let Jesus lug them around for a while because that's what he signed up for. In a way, it was like how you feel so much better after you barf.

I was mostly spared the inquisition, for my sins were juvenile ones. But still it was scary as I'd sit there squirming from all the intimate questions that needed to be asked. My bishop would ask me, straight up, if I was having any trouble with masturbation. The answer was always the same: "Nope, Bishop, not a bit."

22

I WAS SITTING IN THE KITCHEN WITH my little sister, Jane, when the phone rang. We were hunched over a sun lamp, inches away from it with small eyeglasses to protect our eyeballs, getting sunburned on purpose. We were trying to burn off as many zits as we could, our faces redder than fever victims. (This was during my extended Bangs Phase because I had pimples on my forehead, so I grew my bangs down to my eyebrows, like Paul on the Rubber Soul album. I hated the wind during this phase of my life.)

We couldn't be bothered by the ringing phone on the wall and my exasperated mom finally answered it. ("I'm not an octopus, you guys.")

"Oh, hello, Bishop. Leonard? Sure, let me go get him." My mom put the receiver to her chest and yelled for my dad. "Leonard! It's Bishop Jensen."

My dad came in and she handed him the phone. "Uh huh," he said into the receiver. "Sure, I understand. Yes, I think that would be fine. Okay, just a minute, let me put her back on." Then he handed the phone back to my mom.

The bishop wanted to ask my mom to teach the 8-year-olds in Sunday School, but it was incumbent upon him to first ask my dad, as the priesthood holder in the family, for his permission to ask my mom if she would like to teach Sunday School. Once my dad gave him the green light to ask my mom, the bishop was good to go.

Did this annoy my mom, infuriate her? Did she find it odd? Did this blatant display of sexism in the church offend her sense of justice, her sense of equality? No, not really. At least she didn't act like it. That's just the way it was.

At the time, I took for granted my place in the world, an elevated position over women. Indeed, as a 12-year-old boy, I technically had more power and authority in my world than a full-grown woman had. This, unfortunately, did not allow me to sass my mom, but I did have the priesthood and she did not. This never struck me as odd and I tried not to be arrogant about it. I was simply born into a culture where I and my seven brothers would get the priesthood and my mom and two sisters would not.

Gloria Steinem and other feminists who burned their bras to call out the inequality were among Mormonism's least popular people. They were intentionally thwarting God's plan by trying to make a woman's place in the home seem low. And how wicked was *that?* A man's role was to be the breadwinner and priesthood holder and a woman's place was to honor his role. This was so deeply embedded in my brain that I remember believing as a youngster that a neighborhood lady who worked for the phone company didn't love her children as much as a woman who never changed out of her muumuu. Mike's mom, on the other hand, didn't even know how to drive. Why learn? She wasn't going anywhere.

Good Mormon women were willing, if not eager, to prolong their own place in this system. My mom and sisters never pushed back against sexism. If anything, they pushed back against the push backers. The only place I saw a bra being burned was on TV. In my neighborhood you'd be more likely to see a book burning, maybe something like *Coffee, Tea, or Me?* or *A Catcher in the Rye.* Maybe even *Valley of the Dolls.* Those few Mormon women who marched for women's rights were met with derision. "Gol, what's suddenly got into *her?* Is she one of them feminists or something?" So the vast majority of women in our community were complicit in their own subjugation. They joined other Mormon women in saying they were *glad* they didn't have the priesthood because it was too much responsibility. Or they'd make an inside joke of it, saying that even though their husbands technically lorded over them, they were smart enough to outwit the dunce. Let Larry have the priesthood for all I care—we both know who's really in charge.

Of course, Mormons didn't have a corner on the sexism thing. I don't remember hearing about the Vatican stomping its foot and threatening a tantrum until women were ordained priests. And later in life, when I learned a bit about Islam and the fact that women could actually be stoned to death for not covering themselves from the view of men, I definitely thought they were worse than Mormons, by a mile.

But in the meantime, I enjoyed being part of the patriarchy. It was nice to have the priesthood, to feel like I was in an elect, chosen one. Of course, my view of my sex as the superior one wasn't formed exclusively by the Mormon religion. There were newspapers where all the news was about men. There were hospitals where all the doctors were men. There were also the movies where all the heroes and decision-makers were men. Women, even those in leading roles, were relevant only for their beauty and/or their subservience. There was the hooker in *Gunsmoke,* the wife in *Father Knows Best*, and the maid in *My Three Sons*. The only female Hollywood hero in my childhood culture was a dog named Lassie (who was actually a male, but they pretended he was a she for the show).

———————

Everyone, Saint or Gentile, was welcome in our church services. However, if you were a Gentile, your presence would be obvious. Perhaps it would be something about the way you dressed—that your clothes were not quite as modest, your blouse showing enough of your shoulder to reveal the absence of your sacred underwear, or that the spaghetti straps made you look like a common prostitute. Or maybe it would be the absence of a sharp part in your hair, or that you weren't accompanied by a passel of children. And you probably wouldn't be lugging your scriptures around either. There were plenty of ways you'd stick out.

If you had come to one of our sacrament meetings when I was a boy, you wouldn't have seen a woman offer the opening or closing prayer. That task was reserved for a man; someone with the priesthood. The church changed that rule when I was a teenager and I was a bit surprised at the wholesale concession to modernity, the departure from conservative values. People were all abuzz because we didn't change the order of things very often. Women could now pray in sacrament meeting? Holy crap! What next? A female bishop?

Even though my dad had the priesthood, my mom was a lot smarter than he was and I think he would've been the first to agree. He was extremely modest when commenting on his own intelligence and he knew my mom was smart, notwithstanding her lack of a high school diploma. She was a whiz with spelling, reading, current events, and trivia. My dad was not. If they were both alive today, my mom would know who Prince and Lady Gaga were, while my dad would guess they were a royal couple from the Middle Ages.

But my dad did have the priesthood and he used it more than most men. For one thing, he used it to give blessings. Why limit the power of the priesthood to healing the sick? Why not spread it around and give blessings for any assortment of worthwhile things. You were down in the dumps? Blessing. You were struggling to find your way? Blessing. You got fired from your job? Blessing. Important math test looming? Blessing. Your faith was shaky? Blessing. These fatherly blessings were a welcomed staple in my home growing up.

Two other things I remember about my dad. First, he was a spiritual visionary and, second, he was a crier. He'd lay his hands on your head and start bawling from the get-go, prophesying about what he was seeing in his mind's eye, inspired by his prayerful trance. And because he didn't want to take his hands off your head mid-blessing to break the chain of seeing whatever he was seeing, a dutiful sibling would be standing by, hanky in hand, to wipe his tears, and in some cases, his nose.

I recall going through a rough patch and my dad offering to give me a blessing. Even though my faith had nearly evaporated by then (I was in my 20s and hence the rough patch), I was happy to let my dad do what he wanted. I figured that whatever he had to say, it would make me feel a lot better about my future and what I was going through.

My dad was crying hard, his hands heavy on my head, as he prophesied my life would basically suck going forward. Oh, it was dreary. Why he envisioned such a future was unclear to me, for I didn't see a danged thing when I peered into the mystical abyss. Afterwards, I stood from the chair in my parent's living room and my dad hugged me harder than he ever had (and my dad was a hugger). He told me, nose running, that he loved me more than was humanly possible but that he wouldn't trade my future for that of a dog.

A *dog?* What on earth would happen to me, I wondered? Would I get hit by a Mac truck and become a quad? Would Satan put me in a Full Nelson and force me to break all the commandments, one by one? Would I suddenly start to bear false witness everywhere I went? Would I recklessly do something that caused me to be kicked out of my family? Would I wind up on death row? He couldn't say exactly.

This dire prediction of my future, coming from my dad of all people, the one with such bright optimism, the only person in my life who steadfastly believed in me with irrational exuberance, should have shaken me. But it didn't, because by then I'd begun to see his spiritual visions in a new light. I had not lost faith in my dad, the man, but rather in his role as a spiritual juggernaut. I'd come to think he was a bit looney with his belief in the Last Days and predictions of the apocalypse, perhaps even veering toward spiritual derangement. But, oh, how I loved him.

My mom was more orthodox in her beliefs. She believed whatever the prophet said, without exception or apology. The *prophet* was the undisputed spokesman for God, not my dad (with all due respect, of course). In fact, I don't think she bought into my dad's spiritual ideology. She didn't come right out and say it—she didn't roll her eyes when he'd describe the carnage of the Last Days or the precise way in which the prophesies in the Book of Revelations were so obviously coming to pass—but neither did she sit on the edge of the sofa, her face plastered with enchantment, asking, "And then what'll happen, Leonard?"

As for me, I did not give credence to my dad's gloomy prediction of my adult life. And maybe that was when I realized, as much as I loved and admired my dad, that we weren't cut from the same religious cloth.

23

MY FIRST WRITING ATTEMPT WAS A PAPER for a junior high school project. I was 14. The topic I chose was Population Control. I'd been led to believe it was the single greatest threat to humanity. All I knew was that birth control was evil, as evil as it gets, something they'd only do in Babylon, and somebody had to do something about it because there were spirits up in heaven waiting to be sent down to get a body and birth control was thwarting the plan.

How was God supposed to deliver all those spirits to earth to get their bodies if women were taking The Pill? Yes, the Pill was throwing a monkey wrench into the whole eternal system. I didn't ask myself how it was that God could be hogtied like that. I knew he'd parted the Red Sea allowing the Israelites to escape, but I didn't wonder why he couldn't also rescue his new Chosen People from the dreaded effects of The Pill.

My paper on Population Control (which my mother saved, so I can quote directly from it), contained some real scholarly gems:

There is places to live with lots and lots of land where we could quadruple the world's population and still live just fine. So why is there such a great problem?

*The Zero Population people and other birth control groups would cause the extinction of man kind.

*Pollution and high crime rates is not the result of population growth. This is a ridiculous argument.

*Maybe New York, London, and Tokyo are running out of room but that doesn't mean the entire planet is running out of room. Think about how many people we could fit in Canada and Russia that has a lot of open spaces. We have lots of open spaces in Utah too. So it's pretty obvious we don't have a population problem.

*I am strongly against any means of birth control what so ever. It is immoral. Maybe I am just preduciced because I have nine brothers and sisters.

Those were a few of the highlights. However, notwithstanding my commitment to the concept of multiplying and replenishing the earth, I wasn't as gung-ho about it when the chips were down. I'd been in the front yard playing catch with Steve when my parents called me in one late afternoon. They wanted to chat. I was still holding my Wilson A-2000 baseball mitt as I sat on the sofa across from my parents. They didn't seem the least bit upset, so I knew I wasn't in trouble for drinking my mom's six-pack of Tab or anything.

My mom began. "Honey, your dad and I have some great news."

This was a positive start. Maybe we were going to Disneyland again. I looked out the window at Steve who was throwing pop-ups to himself, waiting for me.

"You're going to have another little brother or sister! Isn't that exciting?"

My reaction was immediate and reflexive. I wasn't trying to hurt them. I wasn't trying to cast a downpour on their parade.

But I couldn't help myself. This was a complicated, messy cry. There was the thought of Howard and his self-satisfied smugness that his parents only had six children. There was the thought of all the kids at school who snickered to know there was already a Driggs kid in every grade. Why did we have to be so weird about having so many children?

"Honey, what's the matter? We thought you'd be excited." There was so much sadness in my mom's voice. I knew they were crushed by my reaction. I knew I'd hurt their feelings. But they didn't have to face my friends who thought we were weird enough as it was. I ran down to my room and buried my face in a pillow. My dad came down a few minutes later. He sat on the edge of my bed, combing my hair with his fingers. When my tears finally petered out, he said, "I know how important it is to be liked by your friends, and I understand why you might be embarrassed. When we had Matt, people sort of teased me, too." They did, I asked? Even the grown-ups? "They did, so I think I understand a little bit about the way you feel. But look how lucky we are to have him in our family. I understand you don't know it now, but I bet there will come a time when you'll love your new baby brother or sister as much as we love you."

I felt pretty stupid when I went back outside because Steve saw the evidence of my tears. What happened? Is everything okay? "Yeah, it's nothing," I said. He didn't push it. And, of course, I didn't let him in on the happy news because his parents only had five kids.

I wanted to be like Steve McQueen or James Dean. They smoked cigarettes and drank beer. Of course, I would not lower myself to actually drink alcohol because I wanted to live with my family in the Celestial Kingdom for eternity, but still I was intrigued. Perhaps that is why I drank my mom's entire six-pack of Tab.

I found it in the pantry and bellied up to the kitchen counter. I lined up all six bottles, side by side, like I assumed they did with bottles of beer in The Bongo Lounge next to my dad's office. I opened one with a can opener and took a sophisticated swig, just like they did in the movies. I drank the bottle and opened the next one. I drank that one, and the next one too. It was all rather cultured, ahhing and belching after each bottle as I sat it down next to the string of empties. Gimme another! By the sixth one I was just trying to finish it. They didn't even taste good. Tab? Seriously? Have you tried it?

I was sick all night and decided getting drunk on Tab wasn't that cool.

The next day I walked into the kitchen where my mom was canning fruit. There were bushel baskets of ripe peaches on the counter and she was lifting a rack of empty Kerr jars from a large pot of boiling water on the stove while listening to the Mormon Tabernacle Choir's rendition of *I Know That My Redeemer Lives* on the Magnavox record player. There was the pungent smell of an autumn orchard with too much spoiled fruit on the ground.

She was wearing an apron my sister had sewn for her in Home Ec and there were beads of sweat on her forehead. She saw me come in and set the jars down on the counter. I'll never forget the look my mom gave me that day, cocking her head just so with a look that said she understood why I'd cried over her pregnancy and that she still loved me more than anything in the world. Then she opened her arms and I fell into them, bawling, as she rubbed my back with her oven-mitt-covered hands. It was a spontaneous, full-bodied, shoulder-racking sob with snot and everything. I never said a thing, and neither did she, other than Now, now, now-ing me. She knew why I was crying. She knew it was because I felt awful for being such a wet blanket on her pregnancy (and quite possibly for drinking her six-pack of Tab).

Perhaps my repentant cry was also in compensation for another misdemeanor from the previous Sunday. I didn't confess it to my mom then, but I did feel bad about it.

Part of my responsibility at church was to prepare the sacrament of bread and water before it was passed around to the congregation. This we did in a small private room at the front of the chapel before the meeting started. On that Sunday afternoon, Howard and I were breaking the loaf of bread into small pieces (eating a few slices as we went) when we spotted a trap door in the ceiling of this small room. Hmph, I wonder what that leads to? The parishioners were streaming in for sacrament meeting but the door was closed to the small room we occupied. We took the liberty of grabbing a stool, and popped open the trap door in the ceiling to have a look around. It led to the attic. Howard and I looked at each other. Was he thinking what I was thinking? He was.

We took the sacrament out to other teenagers in the ward who would bless it, and then we sneaked back into the small room and closed the door behind us. The pews in the chapel were nearly filled by then and the meeting was about to begin. We cracked the door and peeked out. No one realized we were still in the small room. We found a bucket next to a mop in the closet and turned it upside down and then put the stool on top of that. It was wobbly but allowed us to hoist ourselves up into the attic. We could hear the bishop welcoming everyone to the service and knew we were in the clear.

The attic was dark but we could make out the parallel joists running the length of the ceiling, 18 inches apart. Straddling the joists, we could make our way around. The only light into the attic came from small cracks around the light fixtures in the chapel's ceiling every 10 feet or so, where the electrician had cut the holes in the sheetrock a bit too big. From where the parishioners sat in their pews 25 feet below, the cracks were virtually impossible to see.

Howard and I hunched over a light fixture and peered down through the crack. We had a perfect view of everything. In fact, I was looking straight down into the ample cleavage of Sister Harding, a paranoid old maid whose eyes constantly darted about as if she expected trouble from an unknown source. She'd always given us the stink eye when we'd walk past her house on our way home from school, as if she thought we'd try to pull something fancy. This made us want to pull something fancy every time we walked past her house.

I found a small piece of debris and dropped it straight down onto her head. She reached up and brushed at her hair, a gray bob that surrounded her plump face like a fitted bedsheet, then looked around to see if someone had flicked something at her. It was the funniest thing we'd ever seen. So, we crawled around and did it to others. One light fixture had a large enough crack for Howard to drop a small dollop of spit right onto Bob Monson's nose. All hour long we picked our victims. The bishop, who sat front and center on the dais facing his flock, must have thought the congregation was suddenly afflicted with fleas as he watched them brush at their hair and shoulders and then look furtively around.

When the service ended, we crawled back over to the trap door. I was the last one down and I was hanging from the ceiling, my feet trying to find the stool, when I inadvertently kicked it off the bucket which made a racket. Howard propped it back up on top of the bucket as I swung from the trap door like I was on the monkey bars. He grabbed my feet and positioned them on the wobbly stool, then held it while I climbed down. We cracked the door and looked out. Ward members were still milling about, their children tugging on their legs to go home. I looked at Howard who was covered with dust and grime. We had to wait for nearly an hour before the coast was finally clear and it was safe to sneak out.

A few weeks later during the Sunday services, all of us boys were sitting on the front pew because that's where we were supposed to sit in preparation for passing the sacrament around to the congregation. Bishop Jensen stood at the pulpit and peered down at us, a proud smile on his face. "Brothers and Sisters," he said to the congregation. "As I look down at these fine young men, I am struck with the overwhelming thought that they are some of the finest young men on earth, specifically saved by God to come down to earth in these latter days. Stalwart in their testimonies, strong in their commitment to the church. Brothers and Sisters, you should be proud of these boys from our ward, for rarely have I seen such a high level of moral turpitude as I see in these fine young men." The audience members smiled and nodded, for we were indeed fine young men, stalwart and true, brimming with moral turpitude.

I nodded along with him, not realizing what turpitude meant (and I presume the bishop and most in the congregation didn't either). But whether he knew it or not, that word described us pretty well, as I discovered when at some point in the future I actually looked it up. [Webster's dictionary: tur-pi-tude; noun. 1. depravity; wickedness. "Acts of moral turpitude." Synonyms: wickedness – immorality – depravity – corruption – vice – degeneracy – evil – sinfulness.]

24

MY TWO-YEAR MORMON MISSION TO SPREAD THE truth was fast approaching and I had some repenting to do. Of course, I could've lied to Bishop Jensen about all my misdeeds and probably gotten away with it, but then what about all the poor people down there in Mexico where I'd been assigned? They needed to hear the pure message, instead of getting it through the filter of a teenager who masturbated and had stolen from Coachmen's.

This Coachmen's stealing business was but one of the things I needed to repent of, and do so quickly, before the people south of the border were everlastingly screwed. After all, I was supposed to save them from their Catholicism and other assorted sins and they might be doomed if the dumb kid lugging the truth down to them from Salt Lake City, Utah was an unholy vessel of our Lord and Savior, Jesus Christ.

Coachmen's Restaurant was a fine establishment. The Country Sausage & Eggs was delicious, and so were their Strawberry Belgium Waffles. And don't even get me started on the Two Pork Chops Special. I had them all, every Sunday morning, for months, without paying for a single one of them. I didn't even leave a tip. Before you write me off as an irredeemable thief, please know that I wasn't the only one with moral turpitude, and I felt awful about it.

As a Mormon male 12 years or older I had to go to Priesthood Meeting every Sunday morning. There we'd dissect the complexity of the doctrine and discuss what we needed to do to prepare ourselves to become a god someday. There was an hour-long break between Priesthood Meeting and Sunday School. We could have used that time to pray, or read the scriptures. We could have used it to visit the shut-ins or contemplate our moral turpitude. But we didn't. Instead, Eric, Steve, Howard, Mike, and I would drive down to Coachmen's for breakfast. This we did knowing full well that we were not keeping the Sabbath Day holy.

Picture us, a well-groomed quintuplet of nice young Mormon boys in white short-sleeved shirts, unfashionable ties, and marginally ironed slacks. Now, picture us filing in to the Coachmen's restaurant on State Street, fresh off a lesson in priesthood meeting on integrity and the love of Jesus, about to commit a string of dreadful sins. We'd scour the laminated menu and order whatever struck our fancy. After our feast, Howard might go to the bathroom and I might walk up to the counter to fetch a toothpick. Then we'd all sneak out and rendezvous in the car, speeding away like Al Capone.

Did this dining and dashing suggest the church wasn't true? Did it mean that the one and only true church on the face of the earth had failed us? That the golden tablets were a hoax? Not to me. I knew the truth of the church didn't rest upon the frail shoulders of a few teenage miscreants. After all, Judas was one of Jesus's right-hand men and I knew what *he* did.

If we went streaking from time to time, running through the neighborhood naked, daring each other to actually do it in daylight, that didn't make me think the church was a sham. The church hadn't urged me to do such a stupid thing, that was Howard. And none of us received an Indecent Exposure out of the deal.

But it was finally time to prepare my vessel, to make it holier before going on my mission. This presented a few challenges. The first step in repentance was to recognize you had erred. That, I learned, was the easiest step. Another crucial step was to make things right. That was much harder.

I had an assortment of jobs at the time. I was an usher at the Salt Palace, a bus boy at an Italian restaurant, and a house painter. (My house painting career was marked with controversy because I was colorblind, but it was part of what kept me busy.)

I'd saved almost $600 for my mission from this hodgepodge of jobs, and one day I peeled away $200 of it in 20-dollar bills. I drove my rusted-out VW down to the Coachmen's Restaurant and opened the door. The bells chimed. I didn't think the FBI would be waiting, that I'd be arrested on the spot, my photograph taken in front of a large ruler, but I was still nervous as shit. There was a burly man with a handlebar mustache. I wished it'd been a woman. Women were usually nicer.

"Um, are you, like, um, the manager?"

"Yeah, what do you want?"

"So, see, um, I've been stealing from you and I've come to pay you back."

This was not what the manager expected to hear from the kid with long hair and corduroys. At least he didn't seem to recognize me, and I was thankful for that.

"I've added it up as best I can and I think I owe about $200. So, here it is," I said as I dug into my pocket and handed over the money. (It occurs to me now that this guy might have been the dishwasher and simply pocketed the money. If he did, I still think I did my share of repenting and the sin was transferred to him. If he didn't, I repent now for judging him so harshly.)

"Were there any more of you?" he asked. "Or were you the only one?"

"Uh, no, it was just me."

I didn't want to throw my buddies under the bus. I didn't want to cozy up to the manager and fork over names and addresses. I couldn't force Howard, Eric, Steve, and Mike's repentance. I had to make a game-time decision and I chose the higher road. But the higher road according to whom? To Coachmen's, LLC? My buddies? Jesus? I wasn't sure, but I believed my own repentance was complete. The burly manager took my money and said, "Listen, kid, if you ever need a job around here, you just call me. Or if you need a letter of recommendation for somewhere else, just call."

I didn't know the moral to this story. Maybe it was a testament to the power of repentance, or a lesson on the ripe fruits of honesty. Or maybe it was just about the forgiving restaurant manager who'd acted like the dad in the Biblical story of the Prodigal Son. All I knew was that there must've been a moral in there somewhere, because there always was.

However, there was probably no moral for the next batch of no-no's. Take, for example, the first time I drank beer. I had been ushering for a Jethro Tull concert at the Salt Palace. This was a marvelous job that paid virtually nothing. After the concert, Steve and a few other guys picked me up in his Bronco. There were two six-packs of warm Coors and the plan was to get drunk. Prior to that I had a pristine record. Not a sip. Not even a whiff.

I stood on the ledge between good and evil (this is a metaphor, for I was actually sitting in the back seat of Steve's Bronco), and

I picked evil. It was one of the first times in my life I'd actually chosen something for myself, which felt good. On the other hand, it was illegal and against the commandment I believed in at the time, which didn't feel so good.

I lifted the tab with a little *psst* and foam spilled out to the top of the can. I sucked up the foam and recoiled. The other guys were watching me, eager to see how the rookie would do. The taste was awful. I almost barfed but pretended like it really hit the spot. I knew people had to develop a taste for these things. I got that. But I was pretty sure I had a bad can, one that had long since expired. So, when no one was looking, I poured it out and grabbed another can. It was just as bad.

I didn't know how I could possibly get an entire can down. But I gave it the old college try and drank about a can and a half. I felt a little buzz. I figured the appalling taste promised to make beer consumption self-regulating because how, I wondered, could anyone drink enough of the stuff to develop a drinking problem?

The problem with drinking those beers wasn't that I got in trouble or even got drunk. It was more the scary thought that I had knowingly, with malice aforethought, broken the commandments. My prior sins had been vague, sins that were not so easily measured. And they had been mostly private ones that occurred only in my head (like lusting, envying, coveting, and things like that). But this was a public, unambiguous sin. I knew the Word of Wisdom was unique to Mormons, so the sin was personal to everything I'd been taught. I hadn't turned my back on the Ten Commandments, I had turned my back on Mormonism. This made it a more intimate and consequential sin to me.

Now that I had sinned, the string of my unblemished virtue broken, I figured I might as well go all in. If I was going to hell anyway, I reckoned I might as well go on a sinning binge. Hey, anybody up for a quick orgy? Who wants to rob a bank with me? Anybody in the mood to rattle off a string of swear words at a strip club? Is there a person you want to eliminate?

I didn't think I was quite that far gone, but I did go on to commit further crimes, one of which got me expelled. That crime was known as The Food Fight.

There wasn't anything in the scriptures that specifically prohibited masterminding the largest food fight in school history, so at the time, it didn't seem as evil as breaking the Word of Wisdom which I'd already snapped in half with that lukewarm can of Coors.

There was a Mormon seminary building across the street from my high school. There was one across the street from every public high school in the State of Utah. The seminary buildings were like mini-chapels with classrooms, and Mormon kids could actually get high school credit for religious instruction. Of course, we weren't taught about world religions, we were taught Mormonism. I had seminary for my fifth period, sandwiched between math and American history. I sluffed my seminary class every day except one. And the one time I *did* go it resulted in the Leonard and Helen Driggs family moving across town.

We were huddled in our fifth period seminary class while the teacher was yammering on about boring nuances of The Book of Mormon. Howard, Eric, Mike, and I hatched a plan for the four of us to strategically sit around the perimeter of the lunch room the following day. We would open our milk cartons all the way (not just the triangle spout), and on the count of three, would throw them simultaneously toward the center of the lunch room and yell "food fight." It was genius.

The next day exceeded all our expectations. Within five

seconds, everyone in the lunchroom was throwing whatever was on their plate at everyone else. Then chairs started flying and tables were overturned. I tried to get out of there but the floor was covered with milk, Jello, spaghetti sauce, and mandarin oranges. I slipped and fell but got back up and headed for the door to the main hallway just as the cavalry from the principal's office galloped to the scene. I was the last one out before they locked everyone in the lunchroom, determined to catch the masterminds.

The entire student body was ushered from the food-strewn lunchroom to the auditorium where the principal sat everyone down and promised to get to the bottom of it. "Now, I'll ask you once, and only once. Who was it!" And wouldn't you know a few girls fingered Howard and (surprise, surprise) me.

My parents were mad. I think what upset them most was that I was supposed to set a good example for all my little brothers who'd be passing through the hallowed halls of Olympus High School. And now this. I was expelled and my dad and I had to go meet with the vice principal, a redheaded man named Mr. Heywood who didn't pussyfoot around. I was contrite as I sat there with my dad in Heywood's office, remorseful as I could possibly be. I wasn't faking it either. Heywood announced my expulsion which I knew was coming, but I didn't foresee what happened next.

"You know, Mr. Driggs," Mr. Heywood said to my dad, "I heard you have several more children who'll be coming to this school. And, to be honest, I don't know that we want them."

There were maybe five seconds of silence before my dad stood up and leaned across the desk. He was generally a pacifist, but I thought he was going to smack old Heywood right in the nose. "How *dare* you say that about my kids. Warren made a mistake, and he's been expelled for it. Fine. But if you ever say another thing like that about my children, you'll regret it. You'd be damned lucky to have my kids here. Do you hear me? You'd be damned lucky!"

My dad was quiet on the ride home and so was I. Now that we had a common enemy, I figured the best strategy was to lie low. I knew my dad was upset, but I didn't know how upset until later that evening. As soon as we got home, my dad and mom took a long drive. Meanwhile, I babysat my younger siblings without even being asked. When my parents returned, they announced to us that they'd bought another house several miles away. It was a nicer house too, and my siblings had me to thank for it. You're welcome.

I felt like The Food Fight incident actually had a good outcome in the end. But I did a bunch of other stupid things that didn't. Take the time I was dating two girls at the same time and bought both of them a red sweater for Christmas. I mean, the exact same one. I didn't do it to be mean, I did it because I was an idiot and they were on sale. I don't know who felt stupider that first day back from Christmas vacation when they were both wearing the same red sweater; Sandy, Pauline, or me.

Was I a bad person for not telling Lisa Randolph that my wad of Juicy Fruit became tangled in her long blond hair during a slow dance at a high school stomp? Was it wrong to walk away and pretend it wasn't me? Is there partial redemption for the fact that the entire second half of *Baby I'm a Want You* was spent trying to extricate it with my teeth, but only making it worse? How about when I dinged Eric's new car with my ski pole and then feigned outrage right along with him at the unknown jerk who'd done it? Or the time I rode Steve's bike into the fire hydrant and the front tire popped and then I parked it in his breezeway when no one was home like it was as good as new? Or the time I hung a moon at the girl in the McDonald's drive-thru window? Or the times we sneaked into drive-in movie theatres in the trunk of the car? I didn't know if that stuff made me a bad person, I just knew I felt like one.

Therefore, it was ironic when the transgression I *didn't* feel bad about actually landed me in the slammer.

My cousin and I decided to take a road trip to Aspen. We left fairly late in the evening and got hopped up on NoDoz given that we couldn't drink coffee. We had a great time there for two days. There were lots of girls and parties. I remained sober. On Saturday morning I decided to head home (my cousin hitched a ride from someone else). We had just been swimming in our boxer shorts and that was all I was wearing—damp boxer shorts. Nothing else. I was speeding near Glenwood Springs, Colorado (at least that was the allegation—I couldn't verify it because my speedometer was broken). A cop pulled me over and asked me to get out of the car. So, I did, because I respected authority.

"Put your hands on the car and spread your legs," he said.

"Uh, I'm not even wearing a shirt or pants."

"Listen, kid, don't you get smart with me!"

So I got out and he frisked me. In my underwear. Maybe it was precinct policy no matter what people did or didn't have on, but he frisked me like I saw cops do in the movies. There I was, wearing only damp boxer shorts and nothing else, standing spread-eagled on the side of the road with my hands on top of the squad car and this guy was patting me down, Dragnet style. Down my bare back, down my bare legs—the whole shebang. As God is my witness.

"Got any drugs in the car?"

I wasn't a lawyer at the time. I was a mere high school student with a 1.5 GPA. Besides, I had nothing to hide so I said no, and you can check if you want. He did. Nothing.

"That'll be $50 for speeding."

"Okay, I guess I can pay it when I get home to Utah."

"Oh, no you don't, smart ass. You pay it now or you're going to jail."

"But all I have is an out-of-state check." I didn't mention it would bounce.

"Then you're going to jail."

"Yeah, right." I said.

Wrong answer. He cuffed me and put me in the back of the patrol car. He didn't even hold his hand over the top of my head when I got into the back seat to protect it from banging into the top of the door frame, a courtesy I thought they offered to all criminals.

"Uh, can I at least get my clothes?"

To his credit he allowed for that and then drove me several miles into town and booked me into the Glenwood Springs jail. Meanwhile, they towed my car to an impound lot next to the jail and left the door open, completely draining my battery, which I figured they did on purpose.

I'd seen enough movies to know I was allowed a phone call. Since I didn't know any lawyers, I used the pay phone to call my dad. One of my little brothers answered. Get Dad, I said. "Make me," he said. Listen, I'm serious, get Dad. It's important. "Okay, but hustle cuz I'm waiting for a call."

Back then a lot of parents thought it might do you some good to spend a few nights in jail. You know, the whole "scared straight" routine. Personally, I didn't think I needed much straightening—I wasn't a hardened criminal—but my dad said he probably couldn't wire the money for a day or two. What choice did I have but to agree? This wasn't a situation where I could've negotiated my way out by doing the dishes.

The jail consisted of a common area about the size of a living room and maybe five or six individual cells. The cells were off a hallway leading from the common area. Four men were playing cards in the common area and I lay down on my bunk with the scratchy army blanket and thin pillow, sans cover.

I was now a certifiable jail bird.

They delivered our trays of food under the door, just like in the movies. I may have been the only inmate in the history of the Colorado Correctional system who refused coffee on moral grounds. There I was, holding firm to my convictions in the most trying of circumstances. Beat me if you must, imprison me, strip me of my dignity and all my worldly possessions, but do not make me drink coffee!

When they turned off the lights it was pitch black—couldn't-see-your-hand-in-front-of-your-face black. I lay there basically waiting to be raped. Finally, there were the sounds of men snoring and I figured I was in the clear. As I lay there, I thought of Joseph Smith who'd also been in jail (several times). He'd been persecuted for righteousness' sake (well, there were the charges of fraud, theft, destruction of property, and accessory to murder, but I figured those were trumped up charges brought by agents of Satan to make him look bad because that's how Satan typically operated).

I didn't think a mob would descend upon the jail in a stampede of thundering horse hooves and try to murder me, like they did to Joseph. This was no longer the Wild West. And unlike Joseph, no church member had smuggled me a six-shooter to tuck away under my mattress. No one was upset with me for secretly marrying their wife, either. If I feared for my safety it had to do with the other four inmates who might have tried to stab me with a homemade shiv, something they'd whittled from the leg of a stool. My mind went to some dark places in those circumstances.

I was finally released when my dad wired the $50. Ahh, all that persecution and then freedom at last! I borrowed some jumper cables from a man who was leery of me, having just come from jail and all, charged the battery and headed for home.

Not long after I got out of lockup, they caught the serial killer, Ted Bundy, in Glenwood Springs and stuck him in my very cell. A few days later, he escaped by sawing a hole in the ceiling and crawling up to the apartment of the chief jailer who was out for the evening, something I hadn't thought of. He then slipped past the jail's skeleton crew and walked out the door. He wound his way down to Florida and murdered more women a few days later. Those were the murders for which he was eventually strapped to the electric chair and executed.

So Ted Bundy and I had more than one thing in common: we were both Mormon and both served time in the same cell.

25

FROM WHAT I WAS TAUGHT ABOUT OUR CHURCH founder Joseph Smith, I was amazed at the diversity of his talents. He was a visionary, religious thinker, architect, banker, general of his own army, best-selling author, candidate for president, husband to over 30 young women, and an underwear designer.

Why underwear? He wanted to create a sacred garment people could wear under their clothes after they'd been initiated into the holy temple rituals. This garment would remind those who'd been initiated of the solemn vows they'd made in the temple. The garment was also a means of protection against sin and danger—a body armor of sorts.

His design was basically a one-piece cotton long john with a union flap in back. The arms extended to the wrist and the legs extended to the ankle. Over time, the design became more modern. Not modern as in *modern*, but the arm length kept creeping up and is now almost to the top of the shoulder and the leg length has crept to just above the knee. Shortly after I came along there was the option to wear a two-piece version, thank goodness. I couldn't say how Joseph would feel about these concessions to modern fashion, but to the extent I thought about it (not much) I figured he wouldn't like them. Nobody wants their design tampered with, especially if it was inspired by God.

From what I heard, some ultra-devout members never took their garments off, even to bathe (they'd take half off, wash that side, and then repeat and rinse for the other side) or to make love which I thought was just plain weird. But most people treated them about the same way Gentiles treated their underwear. Except because they were sacred, we weren't supposed to just toss them in the trash can under the master-bathroom sink when they'd worn out. We were supposed to cut out the small sacred symbols embroidered on the underwear and *then* throw them out. Garments were sort of like the American Flag that way, like they shouldn't touch the ground, although it was okay for us to toss them in the dirty clothes hamper along with our socks.

Like everyone else, I was instructed to wear my Mormon garments next to my skin. I was glad I wasn't a woman, because they had to wear bras and panties *on top* of their garments, which looked sort of funny, like a little boy who wore his tighty-whities on over his blue jeans when he played Superman. When a girl wore her bra and panties on top of her garments it was not the sort of thing you could un-see.

I heard all sorts of stories about the armor properties of Mormon underwear. Take the case in Mormon lore about the guy who was burned to death in a fire. When they found his charred remains, the areas underneath his garments weren't burned, hardly even singed. Or how about the guy who was shot in the heart but the bullet bounced off? The way I figured it as a boy, you could walk in front of a speeding locomotive and come away unscathed. Come to think of it, your head might be bashed in, but the skin underneath your garments would be pristine, not even bruised.

Did I think my dad looked weird in the morning, fixing Cream of Wheat in his garments? Or how about my mom brushing her teeth with her bra and underwear over a pair of long johns? Not really. Steve's dad wore garments and so did Eric's. In fact, it seemed like everyone did. The truth is they were quite comfy.

Only those who had gone through the temple ceremony were allowed to wear garments. I couldn't imagine why anyone else would want to. I figured a Gentile could sneak a pair on, but why? Then again, the truth was I had no idea what a Gentile would or wouldn't try to get away with. I didn't really know many Gentiles. What was important to me was that I was allowed to wear garments once I went through the temple for the first time. That usually happened when boys turned 19. I couldn't remember exactly when girls were allowed to go (but it would have been a few years later).

There were Mormon churches every few blocks in Utah, but there were only about 15 Mormon temples in the world when I was a kid. They were grand, beautiful edifices in keeping with their designation as Houses of the Lord, because that's where Jesus lived when he visited earth.

Anyone could go into a Mormon chapel, but only devout Mormons were allowed inside a temple because Mormon *temples* were a lot more sacred (and private). In fact, temple goers had to pass a strict worthiness test before they were allowed in. This oral test was not for the faint of heart. It wasn't easy. Once a year, adult Mormons met with their bishop for The Test. They had to satisfy him that they were honest in their business dealings, that they considered Joseph Smith to be a prophet of God, that they believed the Mormon church to be the only true church on the face of the earth, that they paid a full 10% tithing (whether they paid it on the net or the gross was negotiable with their bishop), and that they didn't smoke or drink. There were a few other questions, but that was the bulk of it.

If they passed the test, the bishop gave them a temple recommend which looked like a laminated driver's license. Armed with my temple recommend, I could go to the temple where a guard checked me in at the door after verifying my card was up to snuff.

Once inside the temple, I knew I was in that inner sanctum where only the holiest of holies dare tread, those people who had verified their unblemished virtue and moral integrity. We went directly into the dressing room to change into all-white clothes. There were padlocks on the lockers to protect our valuables from theft. That amused me. ("Okay, that did it! We're not letting any of you unblemished people out until we find out who stole Brother Driggs's wallet!")

The temple ceremony lasted about an hour and followed the exact same script every time. Many regular temple goers had the whole thing memorized from start to finish, which I never did. It was basically a re-creation of God's construction of the earth and the chronological journey each one of us was supposed to follow to become kings, queens, priests, and priestesses in the afterlife. For example, the first scene was God and Jesus deciding to go ahead and build the earth so we could have bodies of flesh and bone like they had. The scene after that was Adam and Eve frolicking in the Garden of Eden with only symbolic fig leaves covering their privates. Those important scenes of human history were portrayed by volunteer actors.

When I thought of Adam and Eve, I pictured a handsome couple, maybe in their early 20s, perhaps a couple like Lee Majors and Farrah Fawcett. So I couldn't wait to see the young actress playing the role of Eve. I figured she'd be gorgeous but perhaps a bit ditsy (she'd been easily beguiled by a talking snake, after all), and wearing only a fig leaf. I imagined her, voluptuous, eating a Red Delicious, the juice dripping seductively from her chin down to her ample cleavage. Those dreams were dashed when the woman who played the role of Eve my first day in the temple came out onto the stage. She was a 70-year-old woman with a gray bun. I assumed it must have been the understudy for the real Eve.

The guy who played the snake (the devil) was also an elderly man who seemed rather harmless to me, like an aging neighbor who liked to putter in his garden and play Crazy Eights. Of course, that's what the devil *would* do, he'd beguile you with how innocent he seemed and then *BAM!* he'd have you right where he wanted you. A few years after I went through the temple the first time, I saw that man at a ward Christmas party. "Hey," I said. "Aren't you the guy who plays the devil at the temple?" He gave a jolly laugh and said, "Yep, that's me." I watched him out of the corner of my eye for the rest of the evening, wondering when he'd sneak over to spike the punch, or pinch Sister Henderson on the butt.

We made solemn oaths in the temple. There were oaths to love our neighbors, oaths to keep the commandments, and oaths to give everything we possibly could to the church. I also had to swear that if I violated those oaths (which we all did at some point) I'd proactively agree to administer to myself an awful, violent death, like slitting my own throat, or ripping my bowels out. That was sort of scary, but a bit more fun were all the secret handshakes and passwords. These were the very secret handshakes and passwords that would be required to get into heaven. I loved the cloak and dagger stuff, but I was petrified I might forget the password. And then what? I'd be screwed, that's what. So, I kept repeating it again and again under my breath, trying to commit it to my everlasting memory.

Adult Mormons were encouraged to go to the temple once a month. This was totally different than going to the chapel for weekly services. My parents used to go the third Tuesday night of every month. They'd make a date night out of it. Once they went through the ritual for the first time themselves, on subsequent visits they'd go through the ceremony as a proxy for someone else, sort of like baptisms for the dead. The dead person wasn't compelled to accept the temple rituals on his or her behalf, but I knew if they didn't, they'd never make it to the Celestial Kingdom.

26

I WAS PROBABLY 16 WHEN THE JEHOVAH WITNESSES came to our door. I was horrified. Who did they think they were, traipsing around knocking on doors, pretending to deliver the truth? The sheer audacity of it made me wonder if they were delusional. We let them in, but that was just so we could try to persuade them to join our church instead because we had such unimpeachable evidence of truth when, clearly, they did not. Did an angel deliver golden tablets to their founder? Um, I didn't think so. But fat chance we were going to convert *them*. My goodness, they were so hell bent on trying to persuade us that we could hardly get a word in edgewise.

As my 19th birthday approached, I was repenting up a storm so I could go on my two-year mission to traipse around knocking on doors, delivering the truth myself. I figured I was about a C+ when I weighed my misdeeds on the scales of sin. There remained the hope that God graded on the curve.

I had blemishes on my resumé, but I figured they weren't weighty enough to ban me from this voluntary service. I hadn't done anything that was so nefarious, so morally turpitudinous, that my bishop wouldn't turn a blind eye. And, besides, I figured my Warren Apology Tour, starting with the repayment to Coachmen's restaurant, had been enough to get me over the top, to make me worthy enough to serve, for everyone loves a repentant sinner. I knew all the Mormon hymns by heart. I could quote at least half of the Ten Commandments verbatim, and I paid a full tithing, on the gross no less. This, I believed, qualified me to go to the ends of the earth to tell wayward souls that if they didn't listen to me and join the Mormon Church, they would rue the day forevermore.

I don't know why I fretted over whether they'd let me serve, because the fact was they *wanted* me to go. They recruited me. It's not like I was trying to get into Harvard. In fact, they'd let just about anyone go provided they had an earnest heart, whether they chronically violated their curfew and masturbated, or not. I mean, if Howard could go on a mission, then who couldn't? About the only guys who were held back were the ones who blabbed about having sex with their girlfriends within a month or two of leaving for their missions. (It was so obvious why Stewart's departure date was delayed. I don't know why he didn't just fib a bit, maybe cop to going to second base, or maybe even third, and leave it at that.)

There was an ingenious system that made me *want* to go. I can't count the number of times I heard a mission would be the best two years of my life while I was growing up. But I think I literally heard it over two thousand times.

There were several universally recognized go-to sayings in Mormonism that I heard repeatedly once I turned about 7 or 8. Here were the top five, in order:

1. I know the church is true;
2. I know Joseph Smith was a true prophet of God;
3. I know The Book of Mormon is the word of God;
4. I know that Jesus lives, and;
5. A Mormon mission is the best two years of your life.

Everything after that just blended into your basic Golden Rule type stuff.

There was a fair share of teenage boys who didn't want to go. They were the ones who thought waking up at six o'clock every morning in a strange country to read the scriptures wasn't their cup of tea. They were the ones who thought trying to learn a foreign language was hard. They were the ones who figured they'd miss their girlfriends or didn't want to wear a shirt and tie every day. Perhaps they were the ones who liked to listen to something other than the Mormon Tabernacle Choir or maybe watch some television. For all I knew, they were the ones who thought pedaling a rickety bicycle around all day in the heat, rain, sleet, or snow didn't sound like much fun.

One thing I knew about my mission was that I would be assigned a companion, because Mormon missionaries always traveled in pairs. They explained the reasons for this, which had mainly to do with safety, but I suspected it was primarily to ensure we kept our eyes on each other and made sure our companion didn't stray into a bar, brothel, or some other place of disrepute. It would be tough to get into trouble when you were stuck like glue to some nerd from Provo, Utah who salivated day and night over the nuances of Biblical prophecy and had never heard of Led Zeppelin. Together with some other missionary, always, for two years. I figured they might as well have passed out matching friendship rings. I mean, you'd practically have to negotiate to go to the bathroom by yourself. So, being a Bobbsey Twin might be yet another reason a teenage boy wouldn't want to sign up for two years.

Actually, there were a myriad of reasons why some of my teenage friends didn't want to go (they all ended up going, but if given a truth serum they didn't really want to). They simply liked their life the way it was. Dating. Girls (the frisky quotient was sky high for my buddies, who at that age were at the peak of their lascivious desires). Listening to music. Watching movies and television. Staying current on events (when I came home from my mission, Jimmy Carter had been the president for over a year and I had never heard of him). Driving a car. Eating regular American food. Sleeping past six o'clock in the morning. Having a job that actually paid money. Holding a girl's hand, or attending college.

For those poor boys, a full court press was in the offing. We weren't talking about a gentle little nudge here. The pressure to go, to conform, was brutal. You honestly have no idea.

"But I don't want to go."

"What! You don't want to share the gospel?"

"Uh, not really."

"Oh, don't be silly. Of course you do."

"I'm thinking about maybe going to college instead."

"That can wait. God wants you to go on a mission."

"So."

"But, what will we say to our friends? What will Grandma think? Don't you care about keeping the commandments?"

"Not enough, I guess."

"But God will be so disappointed, and so will we."

When the guilt didn't stick, they brought out the bribe. Take

Bobby Webber's parents. "I'll tell you what," his parents said. "If you go, we'll buy you any car on the lot when you get home. Whaddya say?"

"Even a Porsche?" he asked.

"Well, maybe not a Porsche, but a good one."

"Okay, then, fine. I guess I'll go. But I still don't want to."

If that didn't work, there was always the cavalry, which consisted of the bishop, the relatives, and friends. Even your girl-friend might be enlisted. "Gol, Warren, I love you and everything, but I only want to marry a returned missionary." The pressure!

None of these tactics were required for me. I wanted to go. There was no handwringing. Going on a mission was as automatic for me as sliding from tenth grade to eleventh grade. It's just what you did. It was the proper order of things. I never even thought about it, never even *considered* not going. Of course I was going!

Having repented to the point of overkill, I filed out my application. Would I faithfully serve the Lord? Heck, yes! Did I believe Joseph Smith was the true prophet? I'll say! Was the Mormon church the only true church on the face of the earth? Duh! All my friends were in the same boat, filing their applications and hoping God would see fit to ask them to give up two years of their life for free. Most of us liked the odds.

And then we waited. Where would God call us to serve? It was fairly well understood that God deliberated over each and every one of our personal strengths and weaknesses before hand-picking our destinations. Would we do better with a Scandinavian clientele or a Hispanic one? What would we tolerate better, rats or mosquitos? Did he think it'd be easier for us to learn Mandarin or Cantonese?

Generally speaking, it was an unwritten booby prize to be sent "stateside". Let's just be honest here. South Dakota? Nevada? With all due respect to the good people of Kentucky, there was no cachet in going there in comparison to, say, Greece. Now, I'm not saying the boys that were sent to Topeka, Kansas were spiritually inferior; however, those who were called to be an elect servant of the Lord in Auckland, New Zealand couldn't hide the pride. It just sounded so much more exotic.

My packet finally arrived in the mail a few months before my 19th birthday.

Dear Elder Driggs,

You are hereby called to be a missionary of the Church of Jesus Christ of Latter-day Saints to labor in the Mexico Torreón Mission.

Your presiding officers have recommended you as one worthy to represent the church as a Minister of the Gospel. It will be your duty to live righteously, to keep the commandments, to honor the holy Priesthood which you bear, to increase your testimony of the divinity of the Restored Gospel of Jesus Christ, to be an exemplar in your life of all the Christian virtues, and to so conduct yourself as a devoted servant of the Lord that you may be an effective advocate and messenger of the Truth.

The letter was signed by the prophet. I imagined him pouring over my resumé one last time and then dictating my individual letter to his secretary (I knew he didn't type it himself—I wasn't *that* dumb). I figured he signed it with a flourish, with absolute conviction that he'd nailed it for me. I didn't consider the possibility that it'd been a form letter and his signature had been stamped.

Mexico Torreón met my definition of quasi-exotic. It wasn't as cool as, say, Tahiti, but I believed it was a heckuva lot better than Flagstaff, Arizona (again, with all due respect to the fine people of Flagstaff).

Phone calls were buzzing throughout the geographical boundaries of Olympus High School. "I got my call to Norway!" Not too shabby. "I got my call to Bogotá!" Nice. "I'm going to Peru!" Excellent. "Uh, so, I got my call to Sacramento and I'm super excited." Yeah, I'll bet you are. They pretended to be so thrilled. Of course, friends and family had the good sense to play along. "Wow! Sacramento? That's the best place *ever*, you lucky son-of-a-gun! My brother-in-law went there and he said it was the best two years of his life!" On the other end of the spectrum there were the phone calls from the spiritually haughty boys who'd been called to Thailand, the ones who couldn't wait to tell you where *they* were going.

After some last-minute housekeeping to clean up the few remaining smudges on my spiritual resumé, there was some shopping to do. The first place to go (the only place, really) was Mr. Mac's where you could buy the Two-Pant-Missionary-Special for about $30. They'd even throw in five white shirts and a handful of ties. These were deluxe, indestructible polyester jobs. "Yeah, um, so I'm looking for the Missionary Special?" Excellent, they said. Right this way! I don't recall my budget for this shopping spree, but it wasn't much. I mean, I wasn't going to the prom. I was going to Mexico where I stuck out like a sore thumb with my white short-sleeved shirt, permanent-pressed pants, tie, name tag, blond hair, and blue eyes.

T minus two weeks and counting. Was I nervous? Did I have cold feet? Did my testimony waver at all? No way! I was pumped! Except for the fact that I was already homesick, already missing my girlfriend. She didn't exactly broadcast it, but I knew she was gearing up for her sorority date-dashes. I wasn't stupid, okay? I knew she'd be going out with that Kevin Blount guy within a week. I said disingenuous things like, "I hope you'll date a lot while I'm gone." What hogwash. I wanted her to experiment with a nunnery for two years. But I knew deep down that Cindy wasn't cut out to be a nun. Not Cindy.

Then there was my Missionary Farewell, the church service devoted to the big-send off. I had to give a speech about how excited I was to be going, and how I knew it was the right thing to do (I basically repeated the Five Sayings—see above—like everyone else did). It was traditional for everyone in the ward to congregate at your house for punch and cookies after the church service. This is when you were given those last-minute pep talks. "Get ready for the best two years of your life!"

Getting my missionary haircut was a traumatic experience, as I knew it would be, so I postponed it until the last day. My hair was long, shoulder length, flipping back in a sexy male Farrah Fawcett sort of way. The night before I left, I sat on a three-legged stool in my parent's kitchen while Jane and my little brothers took out the trimming shears. I winced and braced as they sheared me like a Merino sheep. The next day, after I'd checked in with the rest of the troops at the Missionary Home in downtown Salt Lake City, they went around to inspect our haircuts. They said my hair was too long. Too *long?* Was this a joke? Was it even possible to make it shorter? Did they *want* me to look like a skinhead? Yes, they did. I was sent down the street to a barber who specialized in these last-minute missionary shave jobs.

And then I said goodbye to my parents at the curb on North Temple Street. It was awful. They said the strategy was to make it quick and not let the goodbye drag on. Rip the Band-Aid off! So, the three of us pretended I was going to camp for the weekend. Hey, you'll be back before you know it! How exciting! We're jealous!

I turned around and walked into the building where about five hundred other boys with white shirts, ties, and short hair stood around like deer in the headlights, pretending they simply couldn't wait for the best two years of their life.

27

WE STAYED AT THE MISSION HOME IN Salt Lake City for four days. While there, we were given the Mother Of All Pep Talks. They told us we were God's soldiers being sent forth to the four corners of the earth to save souls. They assured us that we were the most noble and elect, specifically saved for the Last Days to convert the world—the Navy Seals of Jesus. And, oh, how I believed them!

All five hundred of us, in our matching white-shirted uniforms, shoulder to shoulder as God's warriors, belting out hymns at the top of our lungs. It felt good.

> *The Spirit of God like a fire is burning;*
> *The latter-day glory begins to come forth;*
> *The visions and blessings of old are returning;*
> *And angels are coming to visit the earth.*

> *We'll sing and we'll shout with the armies of heaven:*
> *Hosanna, hosanna to God and the Lamb!*
> *Let glory to them in the highest be given,*
> *Henceforth and forever: amen and amen!*

There was also a somber speech about how our bodies were vessels of righteousness and if there was anything we hadn't confessed, any lingering sin at all, it was time to come clean. It was now or never. I noticed some fidgeting down the rows and after that speech there was a long line of white-shirted teenage boys that wrapped around the cafeteria walls. They were standing in line for their turn to rid their souls of its remaining transgressions. It was like a telethon. The lines were open and priesthood holders were standing by to take our calls!

I'd never seen anything like it. Boys were bawling, talking about how they'd felt-up their girlfriend a few nights earlier and now they were sorry, sorrier than they'd ever been in their whole entire lives. Indeed, they pretended they hadn't even enjoyed their romps, as if Satan had been behind it all and the dirty (and most unpleasant) deed had been foisted upon them. And now they were revolted, positively *revolted*, by what they'd done! They were laying their souls bare, about anything really, anything that might possibly make them unworthy vessels. A few boys were sent home with bags under their eyes.

Despite a few fading hickeys on my neck, I decided to risk it and not get in line. I hedged my bet with the thought that any remaining sins had been relatively minor, at least in comparison to the biggies, like sexual adventure. Besides, I figured my sinning was largely my own business and, if push really came to shove, I'd take it up with Jesus later.

I will never forget lying in my bunk that first night. I had never been more depressed in my life. It's not that I didn't think I was doing the right thing—it was that I was just plain homesick and the thought of two years, TWO YEARS, was more than I could reasonably take. I was barely 19 and two years felt like the rest of my life.

After our four-day initiation, I was sent down the road by bus to Provo, Utah, the home of BYU and the Language Training Mission. All the boys who were going to learn a foreign language were sent there. We had two months to learn our new language. That wasn't much time for a below-average student with modest intellect to learn anything, much less a foreign language. But I did. And I did it because I knew God would help me. After all, why would he have personally selected me to go to Mexico to convert his children there if I couldn't speak the language? He had faith in me.

We studied Spanish from sun up to sundown. It was the hardest thing I'd ever done in my life, and it didn't help that I was the weakest student in my language class of eight missionaries. It seemed like the others had a knack for it, and I clearly did not. I assumed they'd taken Spanish in high school and then attended a crash course to freshen up once they'd completed their missionary shopping. I could barely say Donde esta el baño, por favor, and it didn't sound quite right when I did. There were several thousand boys there, all of us cramming like mad. Clusters of boys were speaking German, others French, others Spanish, others Tongan. It was like the freaking Tower of Babel.

It was not unusual to hunt for a private spot to pray, to get whatever help you could from on high. I remember opening coat-closet doors to find boys in there praying. There were heartfelt tears shared with each other about our mutual struggle and a common cause of assistance. We were all in the same boat; the jocks, the nerds, the hippies, the dumb, the smart. We were all white, all had short hair, and all wore the same clothes. Everyone was cool. No one was cool. No one cared if you'd been the high school quarterback or were third string clarinet in the high school band.

Not only did we have to learn a language in that time, we had to memorize the discussions. The "discussions" were a set of eight lesson plans which we were instructed to present to prospective converts. They were to be given in a precise order, word for word. No improvising. No going rogue with a bit of contemporaneous chatter. Word. For. Word. So, imagine me trying to learn Spanish at the same time I was trying to memorize pages of text in Spanish. Each discussion was about 45 minutes long and I had to memorize all of them, hardly even knowing what I was saying. It was tough.

The discussions were peppered with anticipated questions that the prospective convert might ask and we learned how to answer them in the most faith promoting way. We learned how to inspire, deflect, testify, and pray. *Oh, that is an excellent question, Hermano Gonzales! Why, you've walked right into my strike zone! Okay, so now do you see how true it is?*

There were testimony meetings every day, impromptu pep rallies of belief where we'd basically pledge oaths of fealty to the church and our sacred cause. We were like the Hitler Youth groups, marching and testifying in lock step. "I know the church is true. I know God called me to be here. I know Joseph Smith was a prophet." If you keep telling yourself something is true, and keep repeating it in public under oath, it will become true. This environment forged a bond, a brotherhood of like-minded boys who were single-focused on something we believed in with all our hearts. It was us against the heathen world and we had God on our side.

My companion in language training was Elder Sandberg, a fabulous kid who was as committed to our cause as anyone else there. But he was miserably homesick. He spent hours on the phone trying to negotiate a way out, a way to go home with an honorable discharge. But his parents wouldn't hear of it. They threw everything they could at him. The guilt, the fear, the punishment, the reward—whatever it took. They sicced family on him, cousins, bishops, and the leader of the language center. If he went home, he would have been a failure to himself, his family, the true church, and to God. The shame would be extreme.

He'd stuck it out for a few more weeks when we returned to our little dorm room on the BYU campus one night and he started packing his suitcase.

"What are you doing?" I asked.

"I'm going home," he said.

"They let you?"

"Yeah. Well, actually, they're sending me home."

"They're *sending* you home?" This was a surprise given all he'd been through in the preceding month. They didn't just "send you home" when they desperately want you to be there. Unless you'd done something horrible.

"Yeah, I've been excommunicated."

It would have been less surprising if he'd said he was actually an undercover Catholic in disguise.

"You've been *excommunicated?*" This was the worst fate imaginable to a devout Mormon. I hardly even dared say the word out loud because it was so . . . so *awful*. It was the sort of word you said in a lower tone, almost reverently, but in a twisted way. Excommunication was an everlasting consequence of sin. It was a burned-at-the-stake sort of punishment, a public shaming that was beyond anything else they did in Mormonism. *No one* wanted to be excommunicated.

"Yeah," he said. "I finally told them I slept with my girlfriend the night before I left home. So, I'm getting excommunicated from the church."

"Gol, I'm so sorry," I said. And I really was.

"It's okay. It was the only thing I could think of," he said.

"What do you mean? What was the only thing you could think of?"

"Telling them I slept with my girlfriend, so I could go home."

"Wait a minute," I said. "You're telling me you didn't sleep with her but you said you did just so you'd be sent home?"

"Uh huh. I don't even have a girlfriend, but it's the only way I figured they'd let me leave."

I begged him to reconsider. I begged him to recant the lie. But he wouldn't budge. He made me promise I would keep my mouth shut and tell no one of his spiritually reckless ruse. I was horrified, but I never said a word.

Elder Sandberg's case was extreme, but not uncommon (the homesick part). I lay in bed at night, counting the days, thinking about my girlfriend and home. And the countdown was sobering. I left on May 25, 1975. The realization that I would be out in the mission field, unable to call home except once a year on Mother's Day for a few minutes, until Christmas, and then an entire additional year until *another* Christmas passed, and then six more months after *that* was unfathomable.

But the days passed. And lest I've painted a picture of abject unhappiness, I must correct it. I was there because I wanted to be there. And I wanted to be there because I knew it was where I was supposed to be.

There was another boy at the language center who lived in Georgia. I didn't know him well because he was in the Portuguese division, but I'd heard his dad had unexpectedly died two months into his mission. Was he allowed to go home? He was not. Now, there was no barbed wire fencing with armed guards in turrets at every corner of the property. He could have escaped. It would have been the story of the year and the entire church would've been abuzz, but he could have done it. I mean, they wouldn't have *shot* him, or put him in solitary. He told me they urged him to stay because his dad would have wanted him to complete his mission. And perhaps that is true. But I just wondered if that boy needed to be home with his family at a time like that, if only for the funeral if nothing else.

On the other hand, I bet I would have stayed, too.

28

AFTER TWO MONTHS IN THE LANGUAGE TRAINING center, I was shipped off to Mexico. I thought I had a pretty good handle on the language until I arrived in Torreón and heard someone speak. *Say wah?* Could you, like, slow down, a lot? This was slightly terrifying.

I was assigned to a Mexican companion by the name of Elder Martinez. He was about four feet tall and had the energy of an Eveready battery. Great guy. Except he didn't speak a word of English. Not a word. We lived in a total dump above another total dump. The windows had been broken out and it was cold (I thought Mexico was supposed to be hot). There were rats scurrying about and I'd never been fond of rats.

I will never forget my first day in Mexico for as long as I live. I still have night sweats about it—it's one of my go-to dreams, like forgetting to study for the test, or going to school in my underpants. We woke at six o'clock that morning and broke out the scriptures to do some light reading for an hour. Then we knelt and prayed by the sides of our beds. I was sorta freaked out because I was worried a rat might collide with my knees on the floor. Notwithstanding my devotion, it was difficult to harness the spirit and really get in the mood with this rodent threat. I mean, I could *hear* them skittering somewhere close. And Elder Martinez silently prayed *forever*. I wondered if he'd fallen asleep on the job. What on earth could be so important? And if it was that important, wouldn't God already know about it? He finally finished with a flurry and hopped up, eager to start the day which presumably would be like every other day—scouring the countryside looking for converts.

We walked down the creaky stairs to the landlord's house for breakfast (this was an all-inclusive resort, apparently). Our landlady was a rotund little woman who dripped sweat over the eggs that she served on top of the rice and beans. For two years I ate rice and beans. I'd figured I knew the ins and outs of Mexican food having eaten cheese quesadillas at Taco Bell, but this was authentic (which, at least in this case, was code for not quite as good). After breakfast we hopped on our rusty bikes and started pedaling around for Jesus, trying to find someone who wanted to be saved. Hardly anyone did.

We knocked on doors for what seemed like *hours*. I finally looked at my Timex, certain it was about time to call it a day. I figured it had to be nearly dinner time. My first day had been grueling but not *that* bad. Yeah, hard but doable. To my horror, I looked at the dial on my watch and saw it was 9:15. Nine fifteen *A.M.!* I thought my watch must have stopped working. But, no, it was ticking just fine. That may have been the lowest moment of my entire life. I didn't understand half of what my companion was saying and I was so tired I could barely keep my eyes open. I had a stomach ache, and I had only 700 days left to go. But I pretended to be loving it.

The next day we met up with another pair of missionaries. They were white (from Bountiful, Utah) and spoke English. I practically wanted to make-out with them. We went to a drug store and they told me they were out of combs. Combs? Yeah, combs, and could I ask the young female clerk for some. Sure, I guess. "Tiene un pene, por favor?" The look on her face. "Pene?" she asked. Si, that's what I want, I said. The problem with my request was that I already had a serviceable penis. Ha ha, that was so funny I almost forgot to laugh. (Piene = comb; pene = penis, and they sound about the same). See what fun we had!

I don't know if it was the rice and beans or what, but my stomach hurt for weeks. I basically had the cramps, like I was slightly effaced and dilated to about a three. I finally decided to see a doctor when the blessings Elder Martinez kept giving me didn't work (I presume he blamed their failure on my irreversible moral turpitude). We pedaled our bikes to the Clinica and I was led into the exam room where I laid on the table like I was supposed to and the doctor started poking and listening to things through his stethoscope. Then he had me sit up. He pulled the back of my white shirt up so he could put the stethoscope on my bare back. He got the shirt out, no problem. But then he tried tugging up my undershirt. The more he yanked, the bigger my wedgy. How was he supposed to know I was wearing one-piece Mormon undergarments? I tried to explain, but my Spanish was only so-so and I didn't know the word for "one-piece" or "long-john." That would never have happened in Utah. Doctors in Utah just knew better.

It turned out my stomach issue was a viral form of gringo maduración. Eventually my stomach would develop a shield of Mexicano protección to the point that I could even gag down menudo (but I put my foot down on a bowl of soup that had a hoof in it. The hoof had been shaved of its hair, but not completely—there were still little patches of it). I figured if Elder Martinez and his blessings couldn't cure it in the short run then nothing would. In the meantime, I consoled myself in the knowledge that I wasn't Job and only had 697.5 days to go.

I got the hang of the language after a few months. (I never got used to the Mexican music, however. It all sounded the same to me. What, they only had one male singer in the whole country, and only one song?) But my language did improve, dramatically. That's what happened when you couldn't speak English to anyone. But it was a struggle those first few months. I'd sit in the sparse living rooms of those Mexican people beneath a picture of Mother Mary and her halo. I'd have a binder of illustrations on my lap and I'd flip through them as I told the story of Boy Joseph being visited by Angel Moroni. They'd have a look of pure bewilderment, not only for the content of my story but also my broken Spanish. Did that blond gringo kid just say that an angel came down to this José fellow's bedroom in the middle of the night with a gold book? Or did he say a ghost came out of nowhere and snuck into the boy's bedroom to steal his stack of gold and take a book on his way out the door? And what on earth was he saying about Jesus sneaking out of his tomb to fly to America? Okay, we got the magic eyeglasses bit, but did he say we'd become Gods if we moved to Salt Lake City?

Despite my failings, we taught a lot of people about the church and many of them joined up. We missionaries in the field were an international sales force, and like any sales force worth its salt, we kept rigid track of stats. We tallied how many lessons we gave, how many hours we knocked on doors, and how many people we baptized. We were ranked according to success. Perhaps it was all those light-bulb sales, or maybe it was my unblemished virtue, but I was good at it. One of the best as it turns out. I was the Tony Robbins of my class! Look at Elder Driggs go, baptizing people left and right! A modern-day John the freaking Baptist!

There was one large house we went to every day for a week. There was an older woman and about 10 younger ones. They all wore enough make-up to have frosted a tray of cupcakes. My companion and I were both young gringos with trim stomachs and were not immune to the attention these girls gave us. "Yep, Elder Thomas," I said, as we pedaled our bikes down the street, dodging potholes, "I think they're on the verge of converting!" And once they were all securely in the fold, we could notch another batch of baptisms on our conversion stats.

I don't know why it took us a full week to figure out this was a whorehouse. They were probably as bewildered as we were. "Are these hombres tan loco? Estos *blind?* I mean, hellloooo. We'd even give 'em a good Christian discount. Geez, we might even give 'em the first one por nada." I'll bet we could have negotiated for a 10-pass punch card at the blow-out price of only 50 pesos a pop to celebrate their conversion. Would it be wrong to admit that I wanted to keep teaching them about the gospel? Wouldn't that have been the good Christian thing to do? I mean, Jesus didn't turn his back on Mary Magdalene, did he?

Despite not converting the prostitutes, we had a lot of success which helped pass the time, and it also helped me get promoted to be the assistant to the mission president.

Like all missions, we had a mission president, the dad of the mission, as it were. It was a job always filled by some devout Mormon man who could afford to leave his day job for three years.

The mission president was responsible for somewhere between two and three hundred young missionaries who were under his (it was always a he) command. Our mission president was named President Wilcomb and he was not without his weaknesses. One of them involved a comely 25-year-old female missionary by the name of Sister Moreno. He met with her all the time, behind closed doors. Sister Moreno's female companion (not nearly as comely) would sit outside the door, twiddling her thumbs, wondering why on earth her companion had to meet with the mission president so often, and for such lengthy sessions. Was her sinning so robust, her confessions so detailed, that it required this much time? Was she possessed by the devil or something?

I was in a tough spot. The other missionaries hadn't been born yesterday and were starting to talk. Was President Wilcomb misbehaving with Sister Moreno? Of course not, I assured them. How could you even suggest such a thing? Sister Moreno is probably just dealing with some family issues, that's all.

But I was worried sick and didn't know what to do. It finally reached the point where I had to do *something* (but what, for I was only 20 years old and he was, like, 50). I prayed my guts out. "Heavenly Father," I begged, "you've gotta do something about this. I hate to boss you around because you're God and all, but I'm telling you, you've got to do something about this by tomorrow. Yeah, tomorrow at the latest. Sorry to give you such a short deadline to work with, but it's come to that. Now, I don't care exactly what you do because you're God, so I'll defer to you on that, but I don't know how much longer I can keep the troops at bay."

I then went to sleep, hopeful that because of my elevated position and religious piety, God had heard the S.O.S.

The next day we received the phone call. President Wilcomb and his 16-year-old son had both been killed in a terrible automobile accident. Everyone was shocked, of course they were, but my reaction was different, for in addition to my shock came the realization that I might have had something to do with his death. I figured I'd killed him, or at least I'd been an accessory to the crime. This was my second kill (don't forget about Sister Ramirez, the old woman who I had killed a few months earlier *during the middle* of my healing blessing). And wait, what about Ryan Wilcomb, President Wilcomb's 16-year-old son? I suppose he'd be on my list of victims too. I liked Ryan—he was a good kid. Did I now have *three* people on my kill list?

What on earth had I done? Was I toxic? Did I have super-human power to kill people, like one of those voodoo doll operators? My God, I felt like the Grim Reaper.

At the time, I honestly believed God had called President Wilcomb home to scold him because of my righteous plea. I assumed God didn't want the important work we were doing to become derailed by a nasty sex scandal. I wasn't too sure about why God had to take 16-year-old Ryan. What had he done wrong to merit this execution?

I figured God knew how important our work was. On the other hand, if he gave a hoot about what we were doing down there in Torreón Mexico, wouldn't he have already known about President Wilcomb's misdeeds with Sister Moreno? Did I really need to fill him in? Was he in the dark about all this until I brought him up to speed? And if I hadn't piped up in prayer would he have allowed this misbehavior to continue? Needless to say, I was troubled by all of it.

I sat through another funeral and heard all the gushing about what a religious rock star President Wilcomb had been. They testified that God had called him home for a higher position. I figured if God had called him home for anything, it would've been to give him a whipping. But I'd decided not to say anything about what I knew and what I'd done to hasten his death, so I just nodded along with the rest of the tearful Saints. I figured it wasn't my place to spill the beans. That's why I'd also kept my mouth shut about all the condoms I'd found in his desk drawer when I cleaned it out a few days after he died. What would have been the point to let loose with that? His wife and family had already been devastated enough.

I knew I shouldn't have judged him, but I couldn't help it. I was mad at him for putting me in such a tough spot and for putting a wrench into the good work we'd been doing. I knew we were all flawed, but I expected more out of him. Did it shake my faith that he, someone I'd looked up to as a man of God, would be so flawed? Of course not. I'd had other examples where the conduct of my church leaders had thrown me for a loop and it hadn't ruptured my faith. For example, when I was a teenager, my bishop was a painting contractor and I was on his crew. I looked up to him because he was the bishop. But I was troubled when we were painting a large warehouse and he told me to dilute the paint. "Dilute the paint?" I asked. "Yeah, mix in about 40% water—they'll never know." I did it because he was the boss, and he was my bishop.

I knew my mission president's raging hormones had nothing to do with the golden tablets. God's true church couldn't be so easily diminished by a combination of President Wilcomb's human weakness and Sister Moreno's comeliness no matter how lofty his church position might have been. The truth was, and only I knew it, if God had given me the green light to pull something fancy with Sister Moreno, I would have given it my best.

In the meantime, I believed God had chosen me to be in Torreon, Mexico to teach people there the truth. And I took that belief to heart, preaching to them like I'd already secured ownership of my own planet. I'd been taught that Mexicans had darker skin for misbehaving in the spirit world before they were born, so I even suggested to some of those I was hoping to convert that maybe one day they could be more like me with lilywhite skin, righteous and pure as can be. All they had to do was join the church, quit with the whole coffee thing, and start paying tithing. I knew it was a bit harsh, but I thought it needed to be said.

My brother Danny served his mission in Brazil before black men were allowed to hold the priesthood. Brazil has a significant European influence combined with a history of slave traffic. Over the years, the races interbred and melded into a rich cosmopolitan culture, but this combination created proselytizing challenges because potential converts were disqualified from holding the priesthood if they had *any* black blood, even a few ounces.

The way the missionary department figured it, it made little sense to spend time trying to convert someone with, say, 8% African blood in their body, because priesthood leadership was necessary to grow and strengthen the church. Of course, people could still join the church if they had black blood, but they wouldn't be able to hold crucial leadership positions. So a policy was developed to smoke out whether the budding Brazilian converts had any black blood.

The missionaries were taught to handle this delicate situation as follows: They would knock on the door of a Brazilian's home. Ding Dong. If invited in, they'd quickly break the ice by commenting on the fact that Brazil is a melting pot similar to the United States. The missionaries would tell them where their ancestors had come from (say, Denmark or England) and then ask the Brazilian family about their own ancestral roots. The Brazilian would usually mention their European roots but not African (because they might have had only a small percentage of African heritage). To further root it out, the missionaries would ask if any of their ancestors came from Africa, or if grandma had kinky hair or darker skin. If they said yes, the missionaries would politely chat for a few more minutes, invite them to church, and hit the road. Of course, the Brazilian had no idea they'd just been scrutinized and categorized. In fact, often times they were left with a favorable impression of these nice young men who hadn't tried to convert them with a hard sell.

I knew from my brother Danny that this racial profiling wasn't done because the Mormons loved the African descendants any less, or thought they were unredeemable. The strategy was simply promoted as a practical solution to a vexing problem.

———

We'd rotate companions every few months or so, and thank goodness for that because I had some real doozies. One was from a small town in northern Utah who was even more arrogant than I was, walking around with a stick up his butt, marveling at his righteousness. Whenever someone would decline our invitation to join the true church, he'd feel compelled to wipe his feet on their doorstep. "What are you doing?" I asked the first time I saw him do it. "I'm wiping my feet on their doorstep so God will know they had a chance to accept the truth and didn't. I'm marking them as cast off from God's salvation." Huh? I hereby solemnly promise that very few Mormons are like that. They might think it, but they would never do such a thing. They'd be more likely to pray for the poor sucker who had a chance at salvation and let it slip through his fingertips.

Once I was clear of the foot wiper, I was stuck with a lad from Twin Falls, Idaho who was so shy he could barely talk. Hey, Elder, this door is all yours (we'd trade off giving the glad tidings, alternating doors to keep it interesting). The door would open and he'd freeze. He was a good guy but I doubted he'd make a living in sales. And then there was my companion from Pendleton, Oregon who didn't like to bathe. I tried to tell him that even John the Baptist got wet from time to time but he wouldn't listen. So, yeah, I met all kinds of guys and they weren't like college roommates I could ditch. But we all had one significant thing in common: a profound devotion to the church.

I learned to accept rejection; doors slammed in my face, rabid dogs sicced on me, people laughing and pointing at me like I was the biggest weirdo they'd ever seen. I wish all those door slammers could have at least known we were trying our best to do what we earnestly believed was right. Even if they didn't believe a word we said, I wish they could've known that we meant well (except maybe the Foot Wiper).

Time actually seemed to speed up as I neared the finish line of my mission. I'd made a lot of great friends and had cultural experiences that most don't get in a lifetime. I had spiritual experiences too; times I felt genuinely touched by something. Was it the longest two years of my life? Definitely. Was it the hardest two years of my life? Without question. Was it the best two years of my life? The answer there is murky.

I'd had the date marked on my calendar for two years: May 25, 1977. A few days before I was to return home, I met with our mission president (a new guy who kept his office door open when he met with sister missionaries). He congratulated me on a job well done. It was time to move on with my life. I hadn't planned on going to college and didn't know what I'd do for a living. I guess I naively figured it would all work out. His final piece of advice was to go home, get married, and multiply and replenish the earth. This is the advice I had expected from him, for that's what Mormons always did, they married and they bred. There may be no better breeders on earth.

I was overcome with emotion when my plane touched down in Salt Lake City. I was finally home, having done my duty with honor. I hadn't seen my brother Danny, my best friend, for over three years, our missions having overlapped. I fell into my mom's arms and then my dad's. Cindy was there too. I can say, unequivocally, that it was the best day of my life.

————

Many years later one of my brothers (a returned missionary himself who remains devout) asked me how much I'd have to be paid to go on a mission again. I asked a series of follow-up questions to clarify the terms. For example, would I have to be 19 again with a girlfriend and raging hormones? Would I have a car? Would I have to re-learn a foreign language and memorize all the discussions again, from scratch? How many people would threaten to beat me up?

After realizing he was talking about the same sort of mission I'd already been on, I settled on $7.5 million. Where that number came from I cannot honestly say, it was just the number I came up with on the fly after considering the hardship. "Would you do it again for $7.4 million?" he asked. No. "Would you do it to end world hunger?" I took the Fifth.

29

I WAS MARRIED WITHIN A FEW MONTHS after I returned from Mexico. I look back now and marvel at my stupidity. I hardly even thought about it. I was going through the motions, once again, following the program. That it turned out so well is a testament to magnificent luck and my wife's infinite tolerance, for by the time I got married, I had yet to use my adult brain.

I wasn't ready to get married. I thought I knew everything, of course, and I still had the flattering notion that I would become a god one day, but I only had 40 bucks to my name, an old end table, a near-fraudulent high school diploma, and I painted houses for $8.00 an hour. I didn't even own a car. I suppose I had potential, like many people do, but I had never lived on my own and had never made a consequential decision in my entire life, let alone one as significant as whether to get married.

Cindy and I were married in a Mormon temple ceremony. My parents, aunts, uncles, and neighbors were there to see it. But my wife's parents weren't allowed inside the building because they didn't have proper clearance. They were Mormons, but inactive ones who couldn't pass the worthiness test (indeed, they didn't want to pass the test). They were good, honest, lovely people, but they didn't pay a full tithing and they drank wine and coffee. So they weren't allowed to see their daughter get married. Instead, they had to wait outside for the ceremony to be completed and then joined the rest of the wedding party for photos in the beautiful gardens of Temple Square in downtown Salt Lake City, suffering the disappointing looks of the more pious souls.

How did I feel about this at the time? Was I outraged that my wife's parents couldn't see their daughter get married? Did I find it the height of gall to forbid them? Did I consider whether Jesus would have been the author of such a policy? Did I find this evangelical blackmail to be unconscionable? Not really. I didn't dwell on it at the time. I figured if they had wanted to see their daughter get married all they had to do was quit the coffee and pay the church like the rest of us.

I'd done group-think my entire life. I didn't consciously do this, at least not during my childhood years. The group-think in my community was to be enveloped in the known certainty of that community's truth. I know many people who find great relief in knowing and I remember when I did, too. With all the other decisions in our lives (what color car to buy, what to make for dinner), it can be comforting to know we don't need to worry about what to believe when it comes to religion. I know from my own experience that it's nice when the beliefs have already been pre-packaged, neatly tied with a ribbon and bow, and delivered to us by the church authorities. My beliefs had been delivered to me that way. The slightly less important beliefs, like whether we could use birth control, have facial hair, or brandish a tattoo, hadn't been hammered home quite as much, but it was still comforting to know someone had all the answers and all we had to do was ask. (Recall my buddy's mom who asked her husband what they believed about the ERA. Or how about the time Sister Sorenson asked her husband what the church's position was on gun control, so she would know what to believe. That's the sort of thing I'm talking about here.)

I'm not a theologian, but I suspect other faiths also excel at pre-packaging a complete belief system with no unanswered questions. Maybe that's the whole point of religion, I don't know. And perhaps a lot of people find this to be a good thing.

So, when did my childhood end? Most people say childhood is supposed to wrap up at about 18, and certainly by the age of 21. Even though my two-year mission exposed me to a foreign culture, however, I believe it may have slightly retarded my personal growth. I say this because most personal growth occurs as a result of the decisions we make. Whether those decisions are wise ones, or not, is almost beside the point—the point is we make them and must assume responsibility for the fallout. I suppose real growth happens more often when we make poor choices because the negative consequences can be so memorable.

I guess we humans make more consequential life decisions when we fly the coop, since that's when we start to challenge authority and the status quo. This is probably true whether we go away to college, join the Peace Corps, or become a ski bum. And even if we continue to live in our parents' basement, we still decide where to work, whether to continue our education, who to hang out with, and what time to come home at night. But the blind obedience of Mormon teenagers is solidified, locked in, at a time when they would otherwise naturally begin to think for themselves and make their own decisions, because that is when they go on their missions. Mormon missionaries make few decisions. Indeed, I hardly made any at all.

I did not decide where I was sent or where I lived when I got there. And neither did I decide what I wore, what I ate, what time I woke up, what time I went to bed, whether I could watch television, what I could listen to, what I was allowed to read, what I thought, who I hung out with, whether I could be alone or tethered to someone (and I mean tethered), what I could and could not do in my spare time, whether I could drive, or what I was allowed to say. I had minimal freedom of speech, movement, and thought.

Some kids might flourish in that environment, but I'm not sure it accelerated my personal growth and development. Many returned missionaries will paint a rosier picture of their mission, extolling the virtues of the controlled environment. I am simply, and honestly, sharing what I myself observed and experienced. And it wasn't all bad. For example, there is no way I would have ever eaten menudo or woken at six o'clock every morning for two years without the discipline required of those mission years. I learned public speaking, leadership, and goal setting skills. I learned to follow rules and to handle rejection. I may very well have flunked college but for my missionary experience. But even army boot camp allows for a few weekend furloughs, and for the chance to make decisions, and mistakes.

Several of my returned-missionary friends promptly enrolled at BYU where their freedom to choose was also checked at the door. As students at this church-owned university they were told what they could wear, the dimensions of their haircuts, and how they were to behave. All students at the university must adhere to a strict Honor Code. Here are a few examples taken directly from the BYU admissions office:

*Alcohol and tobacco are strictly forbidden (on or off campus).

*Strict chastity is required (on or off campus).

*Visitors of the opposite sex are not allowed in dorm rooms except during established open houses, at which time the doors must remain open.

*Homosexual behavior is strictly forbidden. Homosexual behavior includes not only sexual relations between members of the same sex, but all forms of physical intimacy that give expression to homosexual feelings.

*Women's clothing that is sleeveless, strapless, backless, or revealing; has slits above the knee; or is form fitting, is forbidden. Dresses, skirts, and shorts must be knee-length or longer.

*Only one ear piercing per ear is allowed.

*Men must wear their hair trimmed above the collar, leaving the ear uncovered. Sideburns are not allowed to extend below the earlobe. Mustaches must be neatly trimmed and cannot descend below the edge of the mouth. Beards are not allowed.

*Students must obtain a written Ecclesiastical Endorsement for each calendar year verifying they have lived up to the Honor Code. Those who are not in good Honor Code standing will be expelled.

This is not the college experience most Gentiles are accustomed to. My friends, however, were not troubled in the least by this long list of do's and don'ts. "Oh, that's just BYU," they said. "It's no big deal." The Honor Code is as enforceable today as ever, and I wonder whether some of those BYU students are as held back in their personal development just as I was on my mission, with so many of my decisions about who to be and how to live having been made for me.

I was married and at a different university before my childhood ended. It was then, for the first time, that I considered the remote possibility that I didn't have an answer for everything. It was sobering.

I now look at Mormonism differently. My belief in God has become erratic, watered down, and my belief in the church has been washed away completely. While I don't wish the church ill, I no longer choose to defend it the way I used to. For example, I was queasy about polygamy as a boy on some primal level, but I was defensive of any criticism directed at my church. So even though it felt wrong, I was quick to defend it, banishing all my doubts into closets with locks.

I once walked into my office breakroom where a number of secretaries were clustered around a box of bagels and a tub of cream cheese. The Salt Lake Tribune was on the table, opened to a story about a notorious polygamist in southern Utah who'd been arrested for raping a child (his 15-year-old wife, so he said). These devout Mormon secretaries were outraged at this man for his disgusting, sinful, reprehensible conduct. Throw the perverted louse in prison for the rest of his pathetic life!

I didn't say anything to these women, but I had to wonder if they'd forgotten who this man emulated, if they'd forgotten that he took his cue directly from the founder of their church. What was different about this man's conduct from that of Joseph Smith, or Brigham Young? They both claimed they'd been commanded, too.

I was intrigued with these women. I saw this cognitive dissonance as a fascinating snippet of human nature—our fundamental reluctance (or downright refusal) to objectively seek truth wherever it might lead, instead of clinging to beliefs inherited from those who had also inherited them.

I read some research which sought to explain why some people who otherwise demand a rational basis for everything else in their life will ignore the absence of a rational basis for their religious beliefs, as if they have a toggle switch in their brains.

Their determination to believe in those things which bind them together is so strong that they will even die defending it. There are bio-chemists, anthropologists, rocket scientists, and neuro-physicists who are members of the Mormon church. How, I often wonder, do they square their science background with their belief in Angel Moroni, the golden tablets, the War in Heaven, and the mummy scrolls?

Apparently, this research shows that one of the strongest human imperatives is the desire to identify with a group, to belong to a tribe. Mormons are tribal with a capital T. I do not suggest that to diminish their sincerity, or their intellect. But maybe the primitive need to belong to the tribe trumps the intellectual side of the brain. That would explain how even some evolutionary biologists can bend their reason to defend creationism, even in the face of their own research and that of their peers. Instead, they will support the notion that God plopped a fully formed homo sapiens named Adam down into the Garden of Eden approximately 6,000 years ago and then took one of his ribs to make the first human woman, a view their rational brains would find preposterous.

I was a tribesman for the first 27 years of my life. As a young father, despite the fact that my tribal membership was dangling by a thread, I thought it would be good for my kids to be part of my childhood tribe. I went down that road for a while before I realized I was foisting upon them a belief in things that I could not personally support or endorse. Why, I wondered, would I inculcate my child into a club that promoted (or at a very minimum tolerated) values that are anathema to me: sexism, racism, methodical misrepresentation of its history, group-think, polygamy, and the demonization of same-sex attraction? How could I tell them to believe in the gold tablets, the magic spectacles, and the Garden of

Eden (in Missouri, no less) when I could not believe such things myself? They would surely have time in their lives to arrive at their own conclusions about these things. But in the meantime, I decided I would not force feed my own children the ideas I oppose on moral grounds.

Mormons have tried to modernize the church. They've tried to make it seem more mainstream. There is a saying in Mormonism: We Are A Peculiar People. And, indeed, it's true. But Mormons don't want to be *too* peculiar. They want to be popular. They love it when a famous person is a Mormon, especially if he or she is handsome or rich. Do you know how many people told me with self-satisfied pride that Gladys Knight (she of the PIP's) had joined the church? I mean, if that didn't prove the church was true then they didn't know what did.

I was home from my mission and married by the time the church ended its ban on black men holding the priesthood. I didn't jump up and down. I didn't regard it as the single most enlightening thing man had done since he discovered how to split the atom. My reaction was modest surprise and embarrassment that it'd taken them so long. I chalked it up to one more time when God said to ignore his prior revelation because he'd changed his mind. God seems to change his mind a lot throughout the history of Mormonism.

Why, I wondered, should the church be applauded for its belated racial quasi-enlightenment? And neither should I. I hadn't marched for racial justice. I hadn't worn black arm bands in protest. It wasn't *my* ox that was being gored. But I now wish that I had taken a stand for what I believe is simple moral decency. Perhaps the church wishes they had too, if for no other reason than to hide the ugly smudge on their doctrine.

When I look back at my younger self, I wonder how I could

have believed that the skin curse from the War in Heaven was anything more than racist nonsense? On the other hand, how could I not have believed it? I tell myself my early racism was not really mine. I was like most kids. I believed what I was told.

I don't think most modern Mormons are racists. The ones I know are some of the most decent, charitable, and compassionate people on earth. But they have a history, and I went through a period where I felt deeply ashamed of my family's religion, where I hated its racist, sexist, and homophobic roots. I still hate those roots, but I look at it in a broader context now, because I know these human failings existed long before the Mormons came along.

Mormons have a tendency to tinker with their history because they don't want to come off as weird. They want to be popular, like I said. This is why Mormonism's history and its most controversial doctrines have been whitewashed a tad, just a top coat or two, as a concession to mainstream popularity (or to avoid ridicule, black arm bands, and things like that). Take the ban on black men holding the priesthood. Most young Mormons don't really know their church's history. Indeed, they've been led to believe that the church has always been the vanguard of equal rights—crusaders for enlightened moral progress from the get-go. Some might even be tempted to believe the Mormon prophet had his arm linked with Martin Luther King, Jr. down there in Selma, and gave his seat up to Rosa Parks.

I was extremely fortunate to have been born into a community that nurtured me. I am a white male who has enjoyed the benefits that white males have taken at their whim throughout the story of human civilization. Those benefits have not been inconsequential. In fact, I am almost embarrassed to be a white male at times, nearly compelled to apologize for it, as if I personally was complicit in the unequal treatment of women and people of color over the centuries, standing with my foot on their necks while my white brethren and I clung to our positions of power and authority.

No one in the course of human history has had it easier than I have. I know that. But in my desperation to be politically correct I'm uneasy at times—on guard, trying to be modern, afraid of saying the wrong things, because I used to say wrong things all the time. I used the N word as a child. I tried to "Jew people down" before I even had a clue what I was saying. I expressed masculine disgust over same-sex attraction. I did all those things before the advent of video and audio recordings, thank goodness, so I might have otherwise escaped a thorough political vetting if not for my confession here. This confession is not meant to represent moral (or immoral) exhibitionism, but rather a simple truth—that I simply didn't know what I was talking about. I wasn't thinking for myself, and I didn't start thinking for myself for a long time.

———————

I was 27-years old and flying home from a business trip to Chicago. I was in first class and thought I was really something. The flight attendant asked me if I wanted anything to drink. In a moment of unbridled sin and sophistication I ordered a cup of coffee. I sipped it as I looked out the window over the midwestern plains, content to know that I was, indeed, a worldly man.

When I returned home, I told my wife that I'd had a cup of coffee on the plane. I wasn't racked with guilt, but I still felt the need to confess it to her, why I didn't know. We still occasionally went to church, but my faith had mostly deserted me. By that time, I could no longer rationalize a belief in the origin of the church or its teachings. I struggled over the exceedingly long odds that John the Baptist had actually come down from the heavens to teach Joseph Smith how to perform a proper baptism. I figured that Las Vegas bookmakers would have made the existence of the golden tablets a genuine longshot, too. I couldn't imagine what the oddsmakers would have done with heaven-inspired polygamy.

My wife had never been as devout as I was, raised as she was by Jack Mormons who didn't aspire to be gods one day, and didn't appear to give a hoot about the Last Days that were nigh at hand. She'd been a Mormon in Utah to get along, with neither a strong belief, nor the guilt to remain. But still I thought she would find my coffee confession remarkable, even slightly sexy in a bad-boy sort of way. My God, you had a cup of *coffee?* What next? A Harley? A tattoo of Satan?

It was then that the ungodly mother of my children told me she'd been sneaking it for years. It was better for you than Diet Coke, she said. Say what! There was the initial shock and then the amusement that we'd taken these things so *seriously.*

The truth is, both Cindy's and my religious convictions had started to fray years earlier. I think part of it had to do with becoming parents, and having to ask ourselves whether we really wanted to indoctrinate our kids, or have them do their own thinking. They themselves helped us answer this question. Take my son Chad, who was as devout as any other 7-year-old Mormon boy at that age. At the time, Cindy and I were committed to raising good little Mormons. This meant, among other things, that we would be church-goers. It was Sunday morning and we were trying to get everyone up and dressed (perhaps fed too, if there was time) and off to church. Chad was dragging his feet.

"I don't wanna go," he said.

Being the perfect parents that we were, we relied heavily on guilt. "But Heavenly Father wants you to go. He'd be very disappointed in you if you didn't." We had no qualms about blaming this unpleasantry on God.

"But I still don't want to."

"But God wants you to."

"How do you know?" he asked.

"We just do. In fact, you can ask him yourself if you don't believe us. Go into your room and say a prayer and ask God if he wants you to go to church. We're sure he'll say he wants you to."

Chad forlornly went to his bedroom and we forgot about him as we separately negotiated with Scott over what he had to wear to stupid church and Sarah over her hair. A few minutes later, Chad was back. All smiles.

"God said I don't have to go."

"What?" we asked.

"I just said a prayer in my room like you told me to and he said I didn't have to go."

"Huh?"

"Yeah, he said I don't have to."

"Who said that?" we asked.

"Heavenly Father."

What were we to do? We'd taught him that God answered prayers and always gave good advice on these sorts of things. How could we then undermine Chad's claim to have communicated with the divine? Could we trump what God had presumably told him—strip him of his personally inspired communication with the Almighty? And had he really heard from God, or just out-maneuvered us?

If I had tried pulling that stunt as a kid (I'm sure it was a stunt and that God hadn't spoken to Chad in his bedroom that morning; we could hear the Xbox) my parents would have sent me back to my room for another go at it. And they would have kept sending me back until I got the message they wanted me to get.

Cindy and I looked at each other, and then at Chad. "Well, I guess if . . ."

"That's not fair!" said Scott. "Yeah," said Sarah. "How come Chad doesn't have to go?"

We had full-scale mutiny on our hands in the space of three seconds.

Now what? We shrugged our shoulders and accepted the fact that we'd been outwitted. Besides, if I had been honest with myself, I would have acknowledged that God hadn't told me to go to church either. It'd been my parents and community who'd insisted. So, thanks to Chad, we decided to bail on church that week and go for ice cream instead.

Later that evening we went to my parents' house to visit. My mom asked the kids what they'd learned in Sunday School that day. Chad reported that he'd prayed and Heavenly Father had told him he didn't need to go to church. I tried to laugh it off. Yeah, right. Haha. Funny Chad. Then I quickly changed the subject because I didn't want her to know we'd sluffed. I knew she'd tell us that Satan had been behind this rebellion. Because evil prevailed when good men did nothing.

————

I was 28 years old when I took off my garments. It was a personal statement, not a public one, especially coming from a pleaser such as myself. I remember going to one of my children's pre-school programs on my way home from work. I suffered a moment of panic when I pulled into the parking lot and saw my parent's Buick with the familiar dent in the rear bumper. I was wearing a white dress shirt and you could clearly see the absence of my garments if you knew what to look for, the telltale collar under a Mormon man's shirt. Yikes! Would my parents notice? Would they be shocked? Even though it was 95 degrees, I put my suit coat back on before going inside, hoping that would help hide the evidence of my apostasy. Was I so miserably deficient in courage that I dared not reveal my convictions? I must admit that I was. But I didn't want to hurt them with such a flagrant repudiation of what they'd committed their lives to.

And then there was the time in my early-30s (early-30s!) when the doorbell rang. It was my parents coming over for an unexpected visit. The mad rush to hide the coffee maker. Quick, Cindy, stall them at the door! I unplugged it and shoved it onto a shelf in the pantry in the nick of time, the carafe banging against a jar of peanut butter. Can you imagine? You must be scratching your head. You must be telling yourself, okay, that's pathetic. I scratch my head, too.

Mormons claim to have a corner on religious truth. Actually, good Mormons don't believe their church is true, they KNOW it is. And why not? Their doctrines came directly from God himself, unfiltered by their mortal leaders, handed down verbatim. To them, any argument that another faith has sneaked in and confiscated some of the truth is a foolish one. And, of course, they believe the absence of faith is pure madness.

Mormonism praises certainty and disdains doubt. This is the bedrock of Mormonism, the utter celebration of certainty. But might this certainty instead be a reflection of doubt—this insistence that they *know* so as to prevent even the possibility of doubt to creep in? Is certainty a tight gasket to stop any questions before they can even be leaked into the conversation? Or is it a shield to deflect any troubling question from seeping into their midst? A wise philosopher speaking about religious know-it-alls once said: "Frantic orthodoxy is never rooted in faith, but in doubt. Therefore, the more they doubt, the more they are doubly sure."

I have often said that the hardest thing I've ever done—and also the highwater mark on my list of modest achievements—was to leave the church. Now, you might think that is just plain pitiful. Surely there must be more. I mean, how hard is it to figure out the gold tablets weren't real? Geez, Warren, do you still believe in the Easter Bunny, too? Are you convinced that Jack actually climbed the beanstalk? The answer is a perplexing one.

No, it wasn't hard to figure out the gold tablets weren't real, but it was hard to leave my tribe. Real hard.

I had (and still have) significant angst about it. My mom would say the angst was the resulting embers of truth that still burn in my soul because the truth could not be so easily doused. She'd be wrong, though, for the embers are doused, waterlogged actually. If I look deep within myself, there remains no evidence of belief. So why the angst?

As a Mormon, my life was good. Everything was covered, especially my eternal salvation (provided I laid off the Playboy in the bushes outside the ward house). I knew all the answers. I was on a path to godhood. And then I asked a few questions and discovered things I hadn't been told (or hadn't really understood, or even thought about). My belief had been a beautiful tapestry before I started pulling on a few strands, until finally there was nothing but a big messy pile of yarn on the floor. But there had been such comfort in knowing! It was supposed to have all been handled in spectacular fashion! And now nothing. Ugh. I was devastated.

What caused me to pull those strands? What caused me to take my investigation outside the boundaries of Deseret Book (the church's authorized bookstore that sells only faith promoting materials)? Why, if there was such comfort in knowing, did I start picking it apart? Why not leave well enough alone? Why not just revel in my glorious God track? And why, pray tell, haven't others pulled their own threads? And if they have, how do they reconcile a rational belief in Angel Moroni? This continues to be a fascinating mystery to me. It must be the tribe thing.

The payoff for graduating my childhood was deeply rewarding. I discovered a basis for my new beliefs, and it was all mine. This was liberating! But it was scary too, because I felt that I had to re-evaluate everything, for no longer was the answer to everything so neatly pre-packaged. I now actually had to do my own thinking, on every issue, one at a time, and come to my own conclusions.

Once I regained my equilibrium, I paradoxically found more comfort in *not* knowing. Somehow this provided more comfort to me than I'd ever had in knowing everything. It was a relief that conforming belief wasn't required of me—to not just follow the crowd when I knew it didn't add up. The downside was also notable, though. In my community, the automatic default was belief. So I felt like I was on the defensive—as if the burden of proof had shifted to me to establish Angel Moroni *didn't* exist.

I had become the black sheep, the lost soul. How could

Warren *not* believe? Has he lost his mind? And what has he done that is so wicked that he is no longer eligible for a temple recommend? What's that, you say? He doesn't *want* a temple recommend? Oh my, Satan must have him in a head lock. Friends were wary of me, some scattering the way people do when someone vomits and they don't want to be splashed on.

30

OF MY PARENT'S 10 CHILDREN, ONLY Danny and I have left the fold of Mormonism. My remaining eight siblings continue to be devout, perhaps at varying levels, determined in their faith that they are members of the only true church on earth and have found the way to achieve eternal salvation. They are smart, sincere, educated, kind, and loving. There isn't a dumb or whacky one in the bunch. Not one. They accept me and my journey, and I accept theirs. It remains to be seen whether we will all arrive at the same place, or no place at all. In the meantime, I sincerely root them on to wherever their paths lead.

My dad didn't worry about me and my disbelief. The eternal optimist that he was figured I'd be okay, that God knew who I was. My mom was the one who suffered. I honestly believe she would rather have seen me die than lose my faith in Mormonism. I'm serious. I knew this didn't mean she loved me less. In fact, she loved me so much that she would rather have me die (preferably in a quick, painless way, like accidental carbon monoxide poisoning) than live for eternity in the Telestial Kingdom, down there where the non-Mormon hoodlums live. If I'd died a stalwart member, she could have rested knowing I was sitting on the right hand of Jesus. I sincerely regret that she suffered on my account.

How did it make me feel to believe that my mother would have probably wished me dead rather than lose my faith in the golden tablets? It felt all right I suppose, because I think it was a function of her profound belief. It didn't mean she didn't love me. It actually meant she loved me to no end.

A few years before she died of cancer at the young-in-heart age of 75, my mom invited me over to "talk about the church". I knew from many past experiences on the topic that this meant she wanted to bear her testimony to me that she knew beyond a shadow of a doubt that the church was true. True as it could possibly be. I had listened countless times to her testimony, respectfully and without interruption. However, this time I asked her if she would be willing, going into our conversation that afternoon, to consider the remote possibility that I might be right, that maybe I had found the truth. "Oh, honey, you know how much I love you, but I don't think I could do that." You couldn't do what, Mom? You couldn't consider the possibility that maybe something I believed, which disagreed with what you believed, might be true? "I'm sorry, honey, but I know the church it true beyond a shadow of a doubt. I know Joseph Smith was a true prophet. I know The Book of Mormon is the word of God, and I know that Jesus lives. And, Warren, you know this in your heart, too."

I could have been hurt to realize that my mom disrespected my beliefs so much that she couldn't even acknowledge the remote possibility that they were valid. But I wasn't. I knew where I stood with my mom and I knew where she was coming from. So, I drove over to her house that afternoon and listened to her share her truth with me. Then we had a great visit about American Idol, Dancing with the Stars, and what my children were up to. I didn't try to persuade her of anything, for what do I know? Besides, she was my mom. Funny. Relatable. Popular. Modern. Old fashioned. Chic. Backward. Hip. Conservative. There was only one Helen Driggs.

Most everyone loves their parents, of course they do, but mine broke all the molds. A few weeks after they'd both passed away, the 10 of us children met in my parents' living room to divvy up their possessions (and they had a lot of nice things by then).

Inheritance time can be messy between the heirs, even ugly, a raging debate over who gets what. You see it so often it has become a cliché. Our family was no exception, but not in the way you might think. I believe this inheritance debacle over my parent's stuff may have been the greatest tribute to their legacy.

It was resolved that we would draw numbers between 1 and 10, then go around selecting things we wanted, in that order, until everything had been taken. Fair enough. We knew this would take a while, but we had all night.

Julie drew number one. What would she choose? The grand piano? One of the expensive oriental rugs? An antique grandfather clock perhaps? Nope. She chose an old end table in a spare bedroom downstairs. *What?* No, seriously, Julie, what do you want? "I love that little end table," she said. Does it mean something special to you? I mean, you could have anything in the entire house. "No," she said, "not really." Then why not take that oil painting over there? It's worth a lot, we said. "It's okay," she said. "I know Ben has always liked that painting." Okay, then what about that one over there? "It is beautiful," she said, "but Matt and Ali just remodeled their house and I bet they'd want it more."

Steve goes next and it's the same thing. He takes some stupid lamp. We could barely stop laughing at our dysfunction in splitting up their stuff. We were getting nowhere. Or, were we?

It was finally resolved that we would all put our heads down and close our eyes when it was someone's turn to pick, lest we betray our unintended desire for something with a "look" or a cough. And thus, we proceeded, wincing whenever we accidentally selected something nice, hoping we weren't taking what someone else might have wanted. It took all night, a night I will never forget.

I wonder what my parents would have thought. I wonder if they would've been surprised. I doubt it. My dad, who cared nothing for material possessions, would have probably picked the stupid lamp too. And my mom, who had collected all the nice things, would have wanted each of us to have three of everything.

All 10 of us were there the day my mom died; Julie, Danny, Warren, Jane, Paul, Dave, Ben, Matt, Steve, and Andy. She was upstairs in her bedroom where she'd spent the last year of her remarkable life. She had shrunk to only a small version of herself. This enormous presence in our lives had only a few moments left.

One long inhale, and then a pause. Five seconds. Ten seconds. Then an exhale. We all hovered over her, tears dripping to the sheets, willing her to keep breathing and willing her to stop, to end her suffering. Fifteen seconds. Thirty seconds. One minute. Then she was gone. Ben picked her lifeless body up in his arms and rocked her like a child. No one said a thing.

We were all there when my dad passed away too, all 10 of us. He had congestive heart failure and left us, also at 75. He was in the hospital awaiting surgery when Danny stopped by to see him. Danny couldn't have known that dad would crash later that night. When my dad saw Danny standing in the doorway of his hospital room, all six-foot-four of him, he lifted the bed sheet, scooted over in the twin-size bed and said with a smile, "Get in here." Danny left 20 minutes later, never to see him again.

The last time I saw my dad was later that evening when it all went south. Nurses and doctors running in, hooking him up to things and wheeling him to the ICU. I held his hand as they wheeled him away. His bright blue eyes were open, looking up at me from the gurney. He was calm. There was the total absence of fear in those eyes. He knew he was dying and yet there was peace. It was like he was trying to tell me that he'd be fine and so would I, whether I believed in the golden tablets or not, for I always knew that my dad believed in me more than he ever believed in them.

I've talked a lot about my dad in this memoir, but I haven't done him justice, for words, even poetic ones, are wholly inadequate. Optimistic. Happy. Fun. Loving. Non-judgmental. Game. Uneducated. Honest. Generous. Childlike. No, there has never been a man like my dad, and never could be.

Despite my unbelief in the origin of Mormonism and its doctrine, I find I still believe in Mormon people. And I emphatically state for the record that Mormons are not weird (at least no weirder than the rest of us). Most of them are kind, honest, modern, smart, friendly people and I was—and still am—fortunate to be associated with them.

I am the product of unique parents and a unique culture, for I was a Mormon boy. Take away all the angels and visions. Call a truce on all our Biblical tales, Saints and Gentiles alike. Disregard our mutually troubled histories and contradictions. What is left, for me, is a heritage rich in love, adventure, devotion, and family.

Afterword and Acknowledgments

I WISH MY PARENTS COULD HAVE READ my childhood memoir. I wonder how they would have reacted. Would they have been touched, or disappointed? Would they have sympathized with what I now see as my profound gullibility, or would they have misunderstood it? Perhaps they would have been proud at seeing in these pages how they'd stuck to their guns and stood up for what they believed and never wavered. I choose to believe they would have been proud of me, even though they might have winced at spots. I think the wincing would have occurred when the doctrine was simply explained to the reader without the flourish of religious literacy and the filter of faith. In any case, I wish to thank them, wherever they might be, for my life and for their love and faith in me.

My beautiful daughter, Sarah, read the manuscript and wondered why I stopped when I did. "You should have kept it going and told more stories about your adulthood." Perhaps I'll get around to that someday, but for now I have to end *somewhere*. And, as Michael Chabon wrote in *The Amazing Adventures of Kavalier and Clay*, "When the first storyteller, having told the first story, fell silent, somebody sitting there by the fire said, 'Then what happened?' and the Age of Sequels began."

A special thanks to my brother, Dan, who uniquely understands me and stood beside me throughout my journey. Also, to Muffy Mead-Ferro whose editing, insight, and encouragement are impossible to overstate. And, finally, to Cindy who was essentially forced to read the manuscript three times and patiently listen to me ask if this phrase sounded better than that phrase.

64282163R00168

Made in the USA
Middletown, DE
31 August 2019